Fall Asleep

Avoid Sleep Deprivations
Start a Fresh Day

A COMPREHENSIVE GUIDE TO SLEEP WELL

ABDUR RASHID

BOOK DESCRIPTION

Are you always having trouble falling asleep or staying asleep? How many times have you found yourself lying awake at night, wondering why you can't get to sleep? How many nights have you been unable to sleep, knowing that you have a busy day ahead of you, but your body and mind still fail to respond to your needs?

Do you want insight into why this happens, and how you can get a better night's sleep every single night? Luckily, you have found the right book!

In this comprehensive guide, you will:

- Explore and understand the different stages of sleep and how they affect you.

- Identify sleep disorders and recognize their symptoms.

- Be able to ditch sleep medication and use therapy to treat your sleep issues.

- Discover the top 10 tech options to help you sleep.

- Discover how to create a haven in your bedroom.

- Explore how sex helps you fall asleep.

- Learn all the important guidelines you need to know about finding the best pillows!

- Discover how to change your diet to get more restful sleep.

- Learn how to create an evening routine that will help you feel relaxed and ready for bed.

• Discover soothing bedtime drinks and ditch alcoholic nightcaps.

• Dispel the myths surrounding sleep and how they could be hindering your ability to sleep through the night.

• And so much more!

If you believe that sleep is the most important part of your day, then you will appreciate the tips and hints in this book to help you make the most of your rest. Get the sleep you need, and you will wake every morning with a smile on your face, a positive attitude, and a joyful outlook on life. Download this book now and to get some restful sleep tonight!

FALL ASLEEP

Avoid Sleep Deprivations Start a Fresh Day

A Comprehensive Guide To Sleep Well

By

Abdur Rashid

Msc (Public Health) Mcsp Consultant Neuro-Spinal & Musculoskeletal Physiotherapist

© Copyright 2021 - All rights reserved.

The contents of this book may not be reproduced, duplicated or transmitted without direct written permission from the author.

Under no circumstances will any legal responsibility or blame be held against the publisher for any reparation, damages, or monetary loss due to the information herein, either directly or indirectly.

Disclaimer:

Please note the information provided in this book are for educational and demonstration purposes only. We are not providing any professional or medical advice. Each and every attempt has been made to provide you accurate, up-to-date, reliable and complete information. This should not be served as a substitute for consultation or medical treatment and diagnosis of a qualified physician or healthcare provider. There are no warranties of any kind are expressed or implied. All readers acknowledge that the author is not engaging in the rendering of any legal, financial, medical, or professional advice. The content of the book has been derived from various authentic and reliable medical-science sources.
Please consult a qualified professional before attempting any techniques outlined in the book. Please consult a licensed medical health professional without any delay if your signs and symptoms are alarming and need emergency treatment. Do not use any content as a replacement for the treatment and advice given by your physician/healthcare provider

By reading this document/disclaimer, the reader agrees and fully understand that under no circumstances is the author responsible for any losses, direct or indirect, which are incurred as a result of the use of information reading including, but not limited to, —errors, omissions, or inaccuracies.

TABLE OF CONTENTS

INTRODUCTION

We all know good sleep is important. When you fail to get your required rest, then your day begins badly. You feel tired, irritable, and out of sorts and can't wait to get to bed to catch up on some quality slumber, which is okay if it only happens now and then, but when this happens most nights, then something must be done.

When you look after your sleep needs and make sure you are getting quality sleep, you create a bedrock for good health. As the Dalai Lama said, "Sleep is the best meditation," and he knew a thing or two! So, how do you guarantee the best night's sleep regularly? This book is your comprehensive guide to sleep and will help you understand how it works, why you may have problems, and how to treat different disorders without medication.

Does your bedroom beckon to you at night to come and rest your weary head, or is it a dumping ground for the family's cast-offs? Are you sleeping on the right pillow? Does your evening routine help you relax, or is it filled with stimulation that stops you from falling asleep? These questions and many more will be answered in detail to help you become a sleep ninja!

CHAPTER 1

THE MECHANISM OF SLEEP

Sleep happens when our bodies need to rest, the brain switches off and rejuvenates, and then we wake refreshed and ready for the day. That's sleep summed up, right?

Quite the opposite, really. Even after decades of research, the precise reason we sleep is still essentially a mystery. Sleep is complicated and impacts every part of our body and central nervous system, which is why we suffer when we don't get enough sleep. The brain goes into overdrive during sleep to produce hormones and chemicals that regulate the different processes during sleeping and waking periods.

How Does the Brain Control Your Sleep/Wake Cycle?

In the past, it was believed that a specific part of the brain found in the hypothalamus was responsible for sleep. The reticular activating system was the center of the waking process. Recent research has shown that the process is much more complex than previously believed, and there is a whole matrix of structures throughout the brain that govern the activity of waking and sleeping.

What Happens When You Sleep?

The minute you fall asleep, change is occurring in your brain and body. The body temperature falls, energy levels fall and reduce the heart rate and metabolic process, so respiration is shallower. These reactions seem to suggest that the body and mind are shutting down, but what is happening is a dynamic process that is taking the body and mind on a fascinating journey. In just one eight-hour sleep period, we undergo multiple sleep patterns that last between 70 minutes and 2 hours. These stages are essential parts of how sleep works.

What Happens To Your Brain When You Sleep?

For quite a long time, researchers weren't sure exactly why we slept. They knew it was a natural process but couldn't understand what happened to the body and mind during the process. Today we know much more about the impact sleep has on our brains. When we consider the mechanics of sleep and how we close down our bodies at night we can look to evolution for some answers. We sleep at night to keep us safe, away from animals who are hunting. Parents are convinced that their kids sleep for long periods to give mom and dad a break from them.

Whatever the reasons, we need sleep to help our brain work properly.

- **Sleep helps our memory function better.** During your waking hours you make a lot of connections and they aren't all worthy of saving. During the night, your brain will analyze these connections and consolidate your long-term memory to retain the ones that are important. It will also prune back the unwanted information and free up space in your brain. This leads to improved productivity which in turn leads to wellbeing.

- **Sleep helps us deal with negative emotions and memories which can lead to depression or anxiety.** When we struggle with sleep these negative emotions can crowd our minds and keep you awake so the cycle of wakeful nights begins. This means that our focus is distracted by negativity and we can become depressed and stressful.

- **Sleep helps our higher cortical function, which is responsible for multi-tasking.** The most important multi-tasking activity we do is driving. When you fail to get a good nights' sleep and then get into your vehicle to drive to work you are already putting yourself at risk.

It is very important for us to have a good night's sleep to improve our productivity at work and feel fresh/energetic while spending time with our loved ones. Without proper sleep, it is difficult to concentrate, maintain a good mood or in some cases; we put our lives in danger while driving or operating any machinery. Therefore we need to pay attention and understand the basics of a good night's sleep further reading this book.

WHAT ARE THE SLEEP STAGES?

Four sleep stages include three non-REM stages, or non-rapid eye movement stages, and one REM stage or rapid eye movement stage. Research has identified the stages by measuring activity in the brain during sleep that identifies the length and intensity of sleep during each stage.

The First Non-REM Stage or N1

When we fall asleep, we enter the first non-REM stage, which lasts for around an average time of three minutes. This can be referred to as the snoozing or dozing off part of the process. During this stage, the body will experience mild twitching as it relaxes into sleep and prepares to move onto the second stage. It would be easy to wake someone who is still in this first stage, and they will generally wake with a start as they haven't progressed to a more subdued state and are still alert.

During the night, as the cycles progress, an uninterrupted sleeper will spend less time in this first stage of sleep. They will move into stage two quicker as the night progresses.

The Second Non-REM Stage or N2

N2 sleep state involves all eye movement ceasing and the body entering a more subdued state. Body temperature will drop considerably as the muscles relax further. The sleeper can still be woken quite easily, but the mind will produce short active bursts of energy to help prevent this. N2 sleep will generally last for an average of twenty minutes and increase as the cycles progress during sleep. When an average night's sleep is recorded, it is found the sleeper will have spent around 50% of their night's rest in the N2 sleep stage.

The Third Non-REM Stage or N3

N3 sleep is traditionally referred to as deep sleep. The body is further relaxed as we enter this stage of sleep, and the brain begins the process of creating delta waves. These brain waves are believed to emerge from the part of the brain known as the thalamus and range in frequency from one to four hertz. This stage of sleep is also known as delta sleep or short-wave sleep.

This stage of sleep is essential for the body to recover and grow. During this sleep stage, glucose levels are stabilized. The human growth hormone is produced, and the body undergoes overall physical restoration. As the body takes this opportunity to heal, the brain is busy working on its ability to produce creative thoughts and dealing with memories.

REM Sleep Stage 4

This is considered the most important stage of the sleep cycle. It is characterized by relaxed muscle tone, rapid eye movements, and intense periods of dreaming. All mammals experience REM sleep, and the brain and body need to get sufficient levels of this type of slumber.

In REM sleep, the brain energy used exceeds the energy levels used when the body is awake. Brainwaves are faster, and acetylcholine levels, the neurotransmitter that delivers messages to other cells within the central and peripheral nervous systems, are higher.

During REM sleep, the skeletal muscles become virtually paralyzed, and the only movement experienced is the rapid eye movement that defines this type of sleep. This is because the mind will experience the most vivid period of dreaming, and the atomic state of all muscles will prevent us from acting out our dreams and injuring ourselves.

HOW DOES THE BODY REGULATE SLEEP?

When we are considering the length and quality of sleep, it is essential to know exactly how the body works to regulate sleep. Two key drivers are explained below:

1) Sleep-Wake Homeostasis: This is a technical description of why we feel tired and crave sleep. The internal sleep drive function is to regulate the amount of sleep we need based on personal needs. In simple words, the more time we spend awake, the greater the need for sleep is. The homeostasis drive is also responsible for longer sleep when the body needs it, for instance, following a period of poor sleep or traveling.

2) The Circadian Alerting System: During our 24 hours, the body relies on our internal body clock to promote sleep and wakefulness. This clock is regulated by the circadian rhythms we naturally obey and other key external stimuli. Natural light and exposure to sunlight is the biggest influence on our circadian rhythms and tells us when to go to sleep.

In a perfect world, these two key drivers would work naturally, and we would all get the optimum amount of sleep we need to function. This is not always the case, and some external factors are highly influential to both the sleep-wake homeostasis and our circadian system.

Stress and anxiety can stop our bodies' natural sleeping patterns, while caffeine or alcohol will also be disruptive. We are also affected by exposure to unnatural light, which interferes with our underlying systems responsible for managing our sleep.

HOW DO HORMONES AFFECT OUR SLEEP?

When we are considering how to get a good night's sleep, it can be a common mistake to dismiss the importance of hormones. The fact is that hormones need to replenish as we sleep to allow us to function effectively the next day. They provide us with the optimal factors we need to cope with the stresses of normal life. They control our appetite, immunity, and overall energy levels, so if they fail to replenish properly, we are left feeling ill-equipped to face the day ahead.

Various factors affect our hormone levels, which in turn lead to a poor night's sleep. Stressful encounters with our partners, exposure to lights, late-night traveling, and high exercise levels can all affect hormones and cause a disturbing imbalance.

Once we are asleep, our hormones really kick into action. Here is how they affect us as we sleep.

- **The Growth Hormone or Somatotrophin**: This is a peptide hormone that stimulates growth and helps our cells become rejuvenated. This harmone produced in the pituitary gland within the brain and released during sleep. Deficient levels of somatotrophin lead to muscle wastage and short bowel syndrome and growth issues in children.

- **Antidiuretic Hormone or ADH**: Also produced in the pituitary gland, this peptide hormone regulates the body's water retention. Low levels of ADH will cause the kidneys to expel too much water and lead to dehydration and low blood pressure.

• **Melatonin**: Produced in the pineal gland that is situated in the brain, this hormone is intimately involved in our sleep/wake cycle and can be used in supplement form to aid patients who suffer from poor sleep cycles.

• **Oxytocin**: Produced in the hypothalamus, this hormone is both peptide and neuropeptide. It plays an important role in both the childbirth process and male reproduction. Oxytocin plays a more important role for women's health, but it is also playing a role in the male as it is responsible for testicular production of testosterone. Levels of oxytocin control the intensity of our dreams and will generally peak around five hours into sleep.

• **Prolactin**: Also known as the lactotrophic hormone, this important hormone plays an influential role in the human body. Primarily it is known for its role in lactation, or the production of milk, in female mammals, but it is also responsible for over 300 other functions. Sometimes known as the "ancient hormone," it has several roles in perfecting the evolutionary care of progeny. It promotes good parenting skills and plays a major part in the mediation of childcare. Prolactin is also involved in strengthening the body's natural defense systems like immunity and metabolism.

• **Cortisol**: This is a steroid hormone, also referred to as the stress hormone. It is responsible for the natural "fight or flight" response when mammals face stressful situations. The natural levels of cortisone dip just before bedtime and encourage the body to drift off into restful sleep while higher levels in the morning cause wakefulness.

• **Insulin:** Produced in the pancreas, this hormone controls glucose levels and how the body utilizes carbohydrates and fats contained in food. When insulin levels are abnormal, it can cause problems in the body like diabetes and high blood sugar. Low insulin levels can be just as damaging as high levels and can lead to weight loss, fatigue, and depression.

• **Ghrelin**: The cells that line the human stomach are responsible for the production of this hormone. It is most commonly known as the hunger hormone because it regulates our appetite and hunger levels. The higher your levels, the hungrier you will become. It is important to regulate ghrelin levels during sleep, so we wake with a healthy level of hunger, ready to eat breakfast. Poor sleep means our bodies create high ghrelin levels that can make us wake up in the night because we are hungry.

• **Aldosterone:** Produced in the adrenal glands' central cortex, this is not one of the better-known types of hormone. Aldosterone plays a key part in controlling blood pressure and sends messages to the kidneys and colon that regulate the amount of sodium released into the bloodstream. This function plays an important part in cardiovascular health, and keeping levels healthy is one of the key-ways to keep your heart functioning effectively.

Hormones are a key part of the sleep/wake process as they tell us when to sleep and when to wake. Healthy sleep is not only important for our physical health. It is an essential biological function that affects mental health as well.

While there is no consensus explanation available for the reason we sleep, the fact that almost every species of animal on Earth cannot function without it means that it is a fundamental part of healthy living. Put quite simply, without sleep we can't function, and understanding as much as we can about the mechanics helps us address any potential problems.

Our bodies need good sleep, and the diverse ramifications that can arise when we ignore that fact are too important to ignore. If we dismiss poor sleep problems and ignore the consequences, it can be extremely damaging to our sleep and can even lead to serious health issues.

Hormone imbalance can lead to more serious effects, so it is important to recognize the symptoms and address the problem as soon as possible. The Endocrine Society has published studies that tell us that even the smallest imbalances in your hormones can cause life changing symptoms. Lack of proper sleep is a major factor in hormonal imbalance, but other factors also play a part.

Women will experience symptoms when they are premenstrual, pregnant, or experiencing the menopause. Other lifestyle components can throw your hormone balance off kilter like being overweight and a lack of exercise. There are medical conditions that affect hormones like diabetes and an underactive thyroid.

These imbalances can manifest in the following ways

- **Sleep Disorders**: Lack of sleep leads to hormonal imbalance that leads to sleep disorders, so a vicious cycle begins.

- **Mood Swings:** Fluctuations in the cortisol hormone levels can cause depression. Low cortisone levels are also found in women suffering from the disease fibromyalgia.

- **Persistent Acne:** A healthy body helps your complexion look fresh and clear so when your hormones are unbalanced it can cause breakouts. Low levels of androgen hormones can contribute to acne and possible scarring. Most women experience an outbreak of spots right before their period and that's natural but if you are plagued by acne then you may need to increase your hormone levels.

- **Weight Gain**: If you are carrying extra weight this can lead to sleep deprivation which leads to hormone imbalance. This then leads to low thyroid levels which slows down your metabolism which can lead to weight gain. This type of chain reaction can seem hard to stop but getting a full nights' sleep can be the first step to improved weight loss. Hormone polarity can also lead to hunger pangs during the night which won't help your diet or attempts to lose weight.

- **Sweating:** When your hormones are off-kilter it can mean you experience excessive sweating. This is both embarrassing and uncomfortable. Night time or during sleep hot flashes and night sweats may be caused by menopause, but it can also signal a serious hormone disparity. If you are certain your bedroom is at the perfect temperature to sleep yet you are still sweating, then it could be your hormones.

- **Constant Fatigue and Memory Fog:** If you wake in the morning after a full nights' sleep yet still feel tired your hormone levels may be responsible. If you continue to ignore these symptoms, then it can lead to chronic fatigue syndrome.

- **Low Sex Drive:** Your hormones play a major part when it comes to your sex drive. They can cause vaginal dryness and lumpy breasts that are tender to the touch. Throw in a lack of estrogen and you have the recipe for reduced sexual intimacy. If you are experiencing any of the symptoms talk to a specialist doctors like an obstetrician or your gynecologist. What you consider embarrassing is what they deal with every day.

- **Headaches and Migraines:** Another common symptom of hormone imbalance can be painful and debilitating headaches. These will affect your focus and power of decision making. This will make you anxious and depressed which can lead to major health problems.

The bottom line is your sleep is important and you need it to function. The brain and body need to work as one to keep you healthy and alert.

CHAPTER 2

MYTHS ABOUT SLEEP

Separating The Facts From Fiction

Sometimes we are the biggest culprits when it comes to our sleep, and we believe our bad habits are inevitable. If you can bust the myths surrounding sleep, it will be easier to improve the quality and length of your rest. Buying into popular myths can be a major reason some of us find it hard to get a great night's sleep.

Myth 1: You Can Become A Morning Person

How many times have you read an online blog that tells you to get up earlier and achieve more? They will tell you that if you wake up at 4 a.m., you will get everything done by lunchtime and feel amazing and productive. The truth is, we are all defined by our chronotype, which means you are either a morning person, a night owl, or someone in between. Your body is genetically programmed to determine your chronotype, and while it can be retrained to some extent by using sunlight, it is virtually impossible to "become a morning person."

Myth 2: You Can Catch Up On the Sleep over the Weekend

How many people do you know who work like demons during the week and then sleep their weekends away to catch up on their sleep? The truth is that this pattern of sleeping disturbs your circadian rhythm and is referred to as "sleep bulimia." Good quality sleep is only achievable with a regular bedtime and wake-up regime. Of course, if you are feeling tired at the weekend, a couple of hours of extra sleep will help, but it should not be a regular habit.

Myth 3: Eating Cheese Makes You Have Nightmares

This is a common misconception that became part of folklore around the 1980s. When combined with crackers, it can be a perfect nighttime snack. The calcium contained in cheese contains an amino acid that produces melatonin, which aids sleep.

Myth 4: Waking A Sleepwalker Up Is Dangerous

Some people believe that waking a sleepwalker can cause them to have a heart attack or a fatal shock. This is simply not true. While it can be very difficult to wake a somnambulist, you should always try to lead them back to their bed. In fact, the danger of attack for the person waking the sleepwalker is more relevant. Sometimes a sleepwalker will be so shocked to be woken they will attack the person trying to wake them. Try to wake them with loud noises from a distance to avoid any chance of an attack. Remember that leaving someone to wander around the house while they are asleep could lead to serious accidents.

Myth 5: You Swallow At Least Eight Spiders Every Year While You Sleep

Legend says that all of us will swallow spiders who crawl into our open mouths during the night, and there is nothing we can do about it! Children and adults alike have been repulsed by this spider-based "fact" since 1993, when a list of things people readily believe was published. Luckily for arachnophobe sleepers, the truth is that we make so much noise when sleeping that we scare spiders and other bugs away from our mouths.

Myth 6: A Nightcap Helps You Sleep

This must be true, right? It's in the name, so it must be a fact. While having an alcoholic drink before bed may help you drift off easier, it does make the quality of your sleep during the night any better. The term nightcap can be traced back to the 14th century when we didn't really understand sleep mechanics. Originally it referred to a warm cap worn at night to keep the head warm, but then developed into a figurative term to describe an alcoholic drink taken before bedtime. It is thought the term came about as the donning of a nightcap would often be accompanied by a late-night drink.

Myth 7: Some People Don't Dream

Dreams are part of being human. They help us to process the experiences and emotions that we have encountered during our waking hours. We use dreams to create scenarios and imagine what would happen if we did certain actions. This helps us become more creative and solve our dilemmas as we sleep. We know that more vivid dreams occur when we are in the REM sleep cycle, but it is believed most of us dream all night. If someone tells you they don't dream, then they are wrong. We may not remember them, but we definitely have them.

Myth 8: It's Fine To Have Your Electronics In The Bedroom If You Block The Blue Light

Most of us know that the blue light emitted from our phones and devices can disrupt our sleep. This has led to a marketing frenzy of blocking devices in the form of covers, glasses, or apps that diminish the amount of blue light in the bedroom. The only way to ensure quality sleep is to leave your devices elsewhere. Remember the time when we went to sleep without having to check our emails or news feed and still managed to make it through the night? Not checking your phone before you go to sleep may be a hard habit to break, but your sleep will improve immediately.

Myth 9: You Should Never Get Up In The Middle Of The Night If You Can't Sleep

It is also a common belief that when you wake in the middle of the night, the best thing to do is remain in bed and count sheep. Experts accept that relaxing imagery can help you drift back to sleep, but can counting fluffy wooly farm animals really help? Some people swear by counting sheep, but it can be more distracting than soothing. Sleep experts now tell us that if we haven't managed to get back to sleep after 20 minutes, the best thing we can do is get up and engage in a soothing activity until we feel sleepy again. Go to another room and listen to music or read a book until you feel ready to return to bed. Ensure you don't watch the clock as this will make you anxious and prevent you from relaxing.

Myth 10: Yawning Means You Are Tired

When we yawn, it indicates we are tired, right? Well, actually, yawning is more complex than that and is based on brain temperature. Inhaling air through yawning occurs when the brain needs oxygen to increase alertness. Your body also uses yawning to stimulate the lungs and make your joints flex. This forces blood to your head and makes your face feel more alert. We do yawn when we are tired and the temperature of our brain is dropping, but we also yawn when we are bored. This happens because our brain is lacking stimulation and is slowing down, which prompts the body to yawn.

Yawning is also contagious, and sometimes just thinking about it can trigger a yawn. Studies carried out by Baylor University proved that catching a yawn shows a capability of empathy and strong bonding skills. They took over 100 students and recorded how they reacted to various facial expressions, including the yawn. They then compared these reactions to their personalities and ground the more empathy a person had, the more likely they would catch a yawn. While the results are interesting, they are also generalized, so if you don't tend to mirror a yawn, it doesn't mean you are a sociopath or a bad character!

Myth 11: Snoring Is Irritating, But It Doesn't Mean Anything

You know exactly how annoying it can be, if you have a partner who snores. Snoring is caused by a decreased airflow and often occurs when we have a cold or blocked nose. That's a natural fact, and we just have to live with it, but if you are constantly snoring, then you need to seek medical help.

Snoring can be a sign of OSA, obstructive sleep apnea, and if any of the symptoms below accompanies it, you should see a doctor:

- Paused breathing during sleep

- Daytime fatigue

- Lack of concentration or failure to perform simple tasks

- Waking up with a headache

- Dry, sore throat

- Interrupted sleep

- Elevated blood pressure levels

- Irregular breathing during sleep like gasping or choking

- Pain in the chest area

OSA is identified with loud snoring bouts interrupted by periods of silence. Sufferers will often wake when they snort or gasp, which leads to broken sleep for both themselves and their partners.

Myth 12: We All Need 8 Hours Of Sleep

There is no one size fits all number of hours when it comes to sleep. We all need to recognize that the best way to measure how much sleep we need is to listen to our bodies. Some people cope with less sleep better than others do, but there is no magic number to gauge your sleep. It is common sense that if a person is regularly getting less than 6 hours of sleep per night, it isn't ideal. Lack of sleep is not just making you tired. It is also affecting your health.

Myth 13: Daytime Naps Are Bad For You

If you need sleep, then napping could be a great way to re-energize your body. A well planned 20-minute power nap can raise your energy levels without affecting your nocturnal patterns. You can benefit from the same boost to your energy as drinking two cups of coffee, and the effects will be long lasting. Timing your naps is essential, and it is recommended you keep them around the 20-minute length. This allows your body to recharge and rests your mind. Anything more than that will encourage deeper sleep, which will lead to grogginess when waking.

Myth 14: Your Brain Shuts Down During Sleep

Thankfully, this is definitely not true. We still need to function as we sleep, so the brain still manages our basic activity levels. Our brain deals with four stages of sleep per cycle during a full night's sleep and up to 5 cycles per night. Our grey matter is constantly working to keep us healthy even when we sleep.

Myth 15: Lying In Bed With Your Eyes Closed Is Just As Good As Sleeping

Some people believe that resting their brain and shutting off outside contact is just as beneficial as sleep. Imagine like closing your laptop at the end of the day. You close all the programs down, collapse all apps and documents and then shut the lid. Your laptop then remains inactive during the evening, ready for you to use in the morning. Our bodies and minds are completely different to laptops, though, and sleep is a continually active experience we need to function healthily. Closing your eyes for a while is a great way to rest and should be embraced as a healthy activity, but it doesn't count as sleeping.

Myth 16: The Snooze Button Helps You Get More Sleep

When you hear the alarm rings, and if your first thought is to hit the snooze button, you aren't getting enough sleep. The extra time you spend "sleeping" is not beneficial for your body because it is fragmented and broken. There is no evidence significant benefit to be gained from the snooze button and delaying getting up. The best practice is to set your alarm to the time you want to get up and start your day with positive action. Snooze buttons should not be part of your morning ritual!

High quality sleep is as important as the food you eat. If you have a better quality sleep it will lead to a healthy life. Debunking the more harmful myths surrounding sleep will help you understand what is fact and what is fiction when it comes to your slumber.

CHAPTER 3

SLEEP DISORDERS EXPLAINED

Everyone knows what it's like to have a bad night's sleep due to outside influences. Stress, traveling, and hectic schedules can all affect sleep and lead to issues with how much sleep we get, but when this occurs regularly, it may be caused by a sleep disorder.

As with most health conditions, it is important to diagnose and treat these kinds of disorders as soon as possible. Early treatment can mean the issues are dealt with sooner, and the negative health consequences are diminished.

WARNING SIGNS OF A SLEEP DISORDER

Chronic sleep problems will affect sufferers in different ways, it is vital to seek treatment and advice if someone has the symptoms listed below:

- Perpetually taking more than 30 minutes to fall asleep

- Tiredness and irritability during the day following a full night's sleep

- Constantly waking up during the night and lying awake for hours

- Needing naps during the day to function

- Lack of concentration

- Dropping off regularly while doing regular tasks

- Regular changes to your sleep/wake schedule

- Unpleasant twitching when falling asleep

- The need for stimulants like caffeine to keep awake during the day

DIAGNOSING SLEEP DISORDERS

Before you seek medical help, it is important to know as much about your condition as you can. Keep a sleep journal for a week and fill in the entries honestly, with as much detail as possible. Check out the therapy section of this book for a detailed sleep journal you can use to record how different factors affect your sleep.

Once you have kept a sleep journal for a few weeks, you will already know the factors you can change yourself and how to implement them. If your sleep is still not satisfactory, it is time to get a medical diagnosis and identify what particular sleep disorder you are suffering from.

Sometimes sleep disorders are a symptom of underlying medical conditions, and it is important to examine the reasons behind your lack of sleep.

The following medical conditions can lead to sleep disorders:

- Sinusitis, symptoms include blocked nose, tenderness around the nose and cheeks, discharge, toothache, and bad breath.

- Asthma

- Mellitus, a form of diabetes which can be dangerous if left untreated

- Hypertension

- Depression and anxiety

- Parkinson's

There are also several non-medical reasons for sleep disorders, which include:

- Bad sleep habits

- Unhealthy lifestyle choices

- Poor diet choices

- Stressful influence from work or personal life

IDENTIFYING THE DISORDER

There is no stigma attached to sleep disorders. Many people suffer from them, and the treatment is effective and available. Please don't hesitate to consult your doctor if you believe you have signs and symptoms from one of the following sleep disorders.

It is always recommended to understand your symptoms and follow the right advice from a licensed healthcare professional accordingly. Early and accurate diagnoses of a disorder/illness still prevent further complications.

INSOMNIA

This is the most commonly diagnosed sleep disorder that can affect all ages. It is common in pregnant women, especially during the second and third semesters, and it can also affect children. The symptoms of insomnia include waking up too early, poor quality sleep, and issues with remaining asleep for long periods.

Women are more likely to suffer from insomnia as compare to men, and menopause can be a factor in some cases, but both men and women from all walks of life could be affected by the following risk factors that can result in insomnia:

- Elevated stress levels

- Emotional upheavals following a trauma

- Lower standard of living due to low income

- Regular travel to different time zones

- Working irregular hours

- Sedentary lifestyle

RESTLESS LEG SYNDROME

As the name suggests, this syndrome involves aches and pain in the lower limbs that interfere with sleeping patterns. While it primarily affects sleep, RLS is classed as a neurological disorder, and treatment will differ from other sleep disorders. There is no real explanation that what causes RLS, but it is believed that caffeine and alcohol can trigger the syndrome and make symptoms worse.

There is no test for RLS, and it is mostly diagnosed following the description of symptoms from the patient.

All the following symptoms need to be present to reach a definitive diagnosis of RLS.

- Unusual physical feelings accompanied by an uncontrollable desire to twitch

- The urge to move for no reason

- Symptoms are heightened when relaxing or sleeping

- The symptoms alleviate with movement

SLEEP APNEA

Disrupted sleep caused by breathing difficulties defines this disorder. The sufferer will often momentarily cease breathing or wake themselves up with a loud gasping sensation or noisy snoring. This is because the condition is brought on by a lack of oxygen that causes sleep apnea symptoms.

PTSD or post-traumatic stress disorder can lead to serious sleep apnea cases, and veterans and other sufferers of PTSD may experience this disorder. Obesity and age also play a part in identifying people who are more likely to experience sleep apnea and other sleeping disorders.

There are three types of sleep apnea which are:

1) Obstructive: Physical causes are responsible for this type of sleep apnea. The narrowing of the central airway leads to a lack of oxygen, which leads to disturbed sleep.

2) Central: Unlike obstructive sleep apnea, this is a psychological disorder. There is no physical reason for blocking oxygen, but the brain is failing to send the correct signals to the respiratory muscles to breathe.

3) Mixed: This is a combination of both physical and psychological sleep apneas.

How Is Sleep Apnea Diagnosed?

There needs to be a complete physical examination of the patient to establish the factors that can signal this type of sleep disorder. The head and neck may provide clues to aid the diagnosis, while a complete medical history questionnaire will need to be completed. Once the medical diagnosis has been established, a doctor will often suggest a series of further tests to give a more detailed idea of the severity of the disorder and the treatments needed to cure it.

These extensive tests will often require a stay in a hospital or designated sleep clinic so the experts can witness what happens during a full night's sleep. The procedure is called a polysomnogram and includes the following procedures:

EEG or Electroencephalogram

This test monitors brain waves and tells the doctors what kinds of sleep the patient is experiencing. Electrodes will record periods of REM sleep and non-REM sleep. They will record periods of dreaming, irregular movements, and forms of paralysis during the night and how long the periods lasted.

EMG or Electromyography

This diagnostic procedure reveals any muscle dysfunction or problems with muscle to nerve signals. Electrodes are attached to the muscles as the patient sleeps and can reveal which areas are affected by pain, cramping, or tingling.

EKG or Electrocardiogram

This 12-lead test is designed to detect the presence of heart disease. Doctors measure the heart's rate and rhythm and check how healthy the heart is during episodes of sleep apnea.

Pulse Oximetry

When the patient sleeps, a small device measures the amount of oxygen in their blood and how the levels differ during disturbed sleep.

ABG or Arterial Blood Gas

This test can be performed in your doctor's facility or at a sleep clinic. It involves a blood sample being tested to measure certain factors, including levels of bicarbonate and oxygen, the pressure levels created by both oxygen and carbon, and the way these levels affect the quality of sleep.

These tests may seem obtrusive and time-consuming, but they give the experts a bigger picture and help them derive a success-ful treatment plan.

LESS COMMON SLEEP DISORDERS

Narcolepsy

A very chronic condition with no known cure. There are medications and techniques to help relieve symptoms, but the biggest aid sufferers can have support. Narcolepsy can strike at any time, and if you have a strong support group, there will always be someone around to help you.

People with narcolepsy will struggle to stay awake no matter what the situation. Narcolepsy can also be accompanied by a condition known as cataplexy that means the sufferer will experience a loss of muscle tone. This is known as narcolepsy type 1, while other symptoms without the cataplexy are known as narcolepsy type 2.

Other Symptoms of Narcolepsy

- Severe daytime fatigue: Narcolepsy means that sufferers can fall asleep anywhere, anytime, and without warning. People with the disorder can nod off during a lively conversation, at work, or even while walking. They can sleep for a few minutes or up to 30 minutes at a time.

- Loss of concentration and failure to focus

Cataplexy: This loss of muscle tone can occur during periods of intense emotions like happiness or surprise. It can cause the person to suffer blurred speech or weakened leg muscles for a period of a few minutes. Some will experience bouts of cataplexy every day, while others will only experience the symptom a couple of times a year.

Sleep Paralysis: Loss of control and paralysis when falling asleep or waking up is a terrifying symptom of narcolepsy. People with the disorder report that they are aware of paralysis episodes but are unable to control them. This type of immobility mimics the natural paralysis that occurs during REM that prevents us from performing dream activities.

Hypnagogic Hallucinations: Narcoleptic sleep can often include these specific types of soporific sightings. The period between waking and sleeping can be disturbed by visions or sounds that aren't physically there. People with narcolepsy often see vivid scenarios described as living their dreams, or they may experience the feeling of someone in their bedroom.

Circadian Rhythm Sleep Disorder

Your body is affected by the natural internal clock that makes you feel sleepy at night and alert during daytime hours. This condition is known as the circadian rhythm and is a critical part of how we sleep. When this rhythm is disturbed, it can lead to different disorders that affect how people sleep.

Based on the characteristics of their sleep, people can be classed into several circadian sleep disorders.

ASP or Advanced Sleep Phase

This disorder is defined by an early bedtime, followed by a wake-up time in the early morning. For instance, if someone goes to bed between 5 p.m. and 9 p.m. and wakes between 1-2 am. and 5 am, then they can be diagnosed with ASP. Most people with ASP are older adults, and the condition is exceedingly rare in younger people.

DSPS or Delayed Sleep Phase

It is believed that around 20% of teenagers and adolescents suffer from this sleep disorder. DSPS is defined by late bedtimes and difficulties waking up on time.

Non-24 Sleep Disorder

This condition is rare in healthy people and usually affects people with intellectual disabilities or blindness. People with Non-24 don't have the mental ability to recognize natural sleep cues such as sunlight and darkness. They will have less conventional sleeping patterns that they find themselves completely at odds with their circadian rhythms.

ISWD or Irregular Sleep-Wake Disorder

This disorder is defined by broken sleep taken during undefined times throughout the day. People will often sleep three or four separate times during a 24-hour period, and often report being constantly tired.

Kleine-Levin Syndrome

Patients with KLS are often described as childlike, dreamy, and spacey. They will be constantly disorientated and lack normal levels of apathy. The condition is largely undefined, and a proper diagnosis can take four years. The cause of KLS is unknown, and there is no cure. Most patients will experience hypersensitivity to light and noise, while others will become aggressive or irritable. Hypersexuality and binge eating are also symptoms of KLS.

Idiopathic Hypersomnia

This is an uncommon sleep disorder that can be difficult to spot. Patients will be excessively sleepy despite having a good night's sleep and can be affected by the need to sleep at any time. This can cause dangerous scenarios for sufferers, especially when driving or working. The condition is also known as EDS or excessive daytime sleeping and can be extremely debilitating.

Sleep disorders can be misunderstood by people who have no concept of their seriousness. Patients can often be dismissed as lazy, lethargic, and generally worthless. Relationships can be hard to form as intense emotions trigger some disorders, and some people will withdraw from feelings to try to control their disorders.

Some people with sleep disorders can harm themselves and others when their symptoms appear. Sleep attacks aren't common, but they are widely misunderstood. If you believe you are suffering from a sleep disorder, then you must seek a diagnosis and treatment soon.

There is a positive outlook for most people, and sometimes just the most basic of changes will improve your symptoms to help you sleep well.

CHAPTER 4

DOES SEX HELP YOU SLEEP BETTER?

What do you think and consider the two most important things that happen in the bedroom? According to the National Sleep Foundation, the bedroom is all about sex and sleep! But does an activity like sex arouse us and make us feel awake, or does it make us feel sleepy and ready for a good night's sleep?

Does having sex help you get some serious shuteye? The quick answer is yes, it does! When we have sex, some serious hormones are released, and some hormones that stop us from falling asleep are reduced. So, despite being excited and aroused once we stop having sex, we are ready for a peaceful and uninterrupted night's sleep.

The scientific explanation of why sex is good for us and will make us sleep better

- **Endorphin:** This hormone is also known as the body's natural painkiller and is released when we need to relieve pain. When we have sex, we experience the release of endorphins that make us feel tranquil and happy.

- **Oxytocin:** This hormone is known as the love hormone and is released when we experience bonding scenarios. When we cuddle our pets or talk to our children, the hormone is released into our central system and makes us feel attached and loved. Sex could be described as the ultimate bonding scenario and leads to a high level of oxytocin being released that makes us feel calm and free from stress. These feelings encourage us to fall asleep naturally without worrying about our daily stresses.

- **Cortisol:** Known as the stress hormone, cortisol is responsible for releasing energy when our bodies are feeling threatened. It raises the levels of glucose in our bloodstream, which results in higher energy levels. This is not good news for people who want to go to sleep, right? The great news is that sex lowers cortisol levels in your system and allows you to sleep deeply and peacefully.

- **Prolactin:** If you orgasm during sex, your body will be flooded with prolactin hormone. This makes our body feel satisfied and content and ready to drift off.

So, if we know that sex before sleep improves our night's rest, why aren't more of us doing it? Mostly because sleep deprivation is one of the key reasons we don't feel in the mood for sex. When this happens, we can get stuck on a giant hamster wheel of sleep deprivation leading to lack of libido, which in turn leads to bad sleep. So how do we get off this wheel? Have sex! Even if you don't particularly feel like it, get back on board and step off that hamster wheel of despair.

Even if the mechanics of sex are less than perfect just spending time with your partner snuggled up under the covers will help you relax. Snuggling releases important hormones and helps us feel safe and secure. If you spend your day avoiding all the things that make you anxious or hinder your sleep then the chances are you will feel relaxed and ready to make love with your partner or yourself.

Set the scene: Make your bedroom a haven for love and romance with candles or low lighting. Play soft ballads in the background and make your partner feel special. Dress to impress! Not everybody likes sweat clothes or pajamas so when you make an effort with your nightclothes it can signal you are ready to get frisky. Sexy nightwear can be uncomfortable but with any luck, it will end up on the bedroom floor and stay there all night.

Make sure you have more than enough time to get intimate and choose a time you aren't going to get interrupted. Good sex can happen whenever you like, and it will still help you sleep. Sex bonds us with our partners and makes us feel relaxed, energized, and happy which all aids sleep.

HOW TO REPLACE SEX WITH INTIMACY

If you are single or maybe you aren't interested in the physical side of relationships, how do you replace sex as an aid for sleep? The answer is all around you. Intimacy is part of relationships outside the traditional idea of partnerships. We all need to feel connected and nurturing the interactions we have with others help us sleep at night.

Intimacy means different things to certain people and here are some ways you can increase levels and promote emotional well-being:

- **Emotional Intimacy:** If you are guarded with your emotions and inflict a barrier between yourself and others, then it could be time to let them in. Think of it as letting your guard down and reaching out to other people emotionally. Share your fears and hopes with the people you trust and build those levels of intimacy. When you arrive home with worries on your mind, pick up the phone and talk to someone. This will help you share your burden and cast it off before you go to bed.
- **Intellectual Intimacy:** Have you ever become overly enthusiastic when you realize someone else has the same weird interest you have? There is a spark as you bounce ideas and share knowledge with them, and you can feel like there are only the two of you in a crowded room. Geeky? Maybe, but we all need intellectual stimulation just as much as we need physical touch, more so for

some people.

Join groups of like-minded people online to discuss your passion and you will feel connected to someone. This is a great way to engage and exercise your brain and aid restful sleep. Remember how good it felt to have deep philosophical discussions in class that made you feel like you had a voice? Revisit that feeling and get talking!

- **Experiential Intimacy:** You build this type of intimacy by spending time with people who love to do the things you love. You share experiences and form bonds as you share your mutual love. This can be as diverse as a passion for board games or love of visiting art galleries. Companionship makes most experiences better, especially when your companion is as passionate as you are about the experience.
- **Spiritual Intimacy:** This is generally about a belief that something beyond the physical realm is out there and it can take many forms. If you have a spiritual belief, choose to reach out to groups of people who believe in your form of spirituality.

Remember intimacy isn't immediate it needs to be built. Put the time into your relationships and the benefits will be with you for life. Our connections help us feel healthy which leads to better sleep, which leads to better health. At last, a circle of actions that promote overall well-being. Intimacy should be a part of all our lives, so start working on yours right now.

CHAPTER 5

HOW TO MAKE
YOUR BEDROOM

A Haven for Sleep

Do you love your bedroom? Is it a welcoming place to retreat to whenever you feel the strains of the day begin to take their toll? Sometimes it can be easy to turn your haven of sleep into the central part of your home. If you are trying to get some time to yourself or sleep in at the weekend, you need to know your bedroom is a place where you can expect to relax without interruptions.

ESTABLISH
BEDROOM RULES

If you have partner, kids or live with roommates, they may not know how to respect your boundaries. This needs to be remedied before you begin transforming your personal space into a haven. Keep it light but make sure they understand just how serious you are.

Try a notice that looks like this:

Hey there!

This bedroom is now a special place for the people who sleep here! We love you all, but we need our space. Please knock before you come in or, even better, wait for us to leave the bedroom!

We know you love our company just like we love yours but imagine how awesome we will be with a bit more sleep! Please respect our wishes and let us get some quality time to ourselves.

Many Thanks, xx

DECLUTTER YOUR ROOM

◆ ◆ ◆

When you enter your bedroom, what emotions do you feel? Are you relaxed, calm, and chilled, or are you completely distracted by all the clutter and mess? Now is the time to get serious about your personal space and make it beautiful.

First, it's time to get rid of all the stuff that doesn't belong there; kids' toys, clothes, or shoes. Random stuff that gets put in your room because there is no room anywhere else. This can include suitcases full of unseasonal clothes or even redundant kitchen paraphernalia and if it doesn't add to the ambiance of your room, get rid of it!

Now deal with the stuff that does belong there but needs organizing. Empty all closet space and sort it out into keep, donate, and trash piles. Be prepared for this to take a good amount of time, and it is important to get it done in one hit. Make sure you have plenty of trash/bin bags, labels, and a clear idea of what your objectives are.

Sort your shoes, jewelry, accessories, and knick-knacks from the top of your nightstand, and make sure you empty the drawers as well. Only keep the stuff you love and make sure you get rid of stuff that is not useful.

Now it's time to tackle underneath the bed or the items you store inside the bed. Make sure all the boxes and suitcases you have shoved away out of sight are dealt with. Be brutal about your choices, and if you feel yourself starting to waver, just imagine all the fun you are going to have when you redecorate these blank spaces. Imagine the cool soft furnishings and funky accessories your new space will have.

Wipe down all the surfaces and vacuum thoroughly. Make sure you clean all your light fittings, switches, and other neglected spaces. If you have any fan in your bedroom, chances are it needs dusting so, take it apart and clean all the individual elements. Now you will know better and have an idea of how much attention your room needs to make it into an oasis of calm.

PLAN A SHOPPING TRIP

Does your bedroom need a coat of paint, or will some tasteful artwork and accessories suffice? Make a detailed list of what you need before you start dressing your bedroom. Do you need a new bed? Maybe your mattress is old and uncomfortable. If you can afford it, splash some cash on your bed and make it as luxurious as possible.

Your bed should be a statement piece. Luckily, big beds are on-trend at the moment, and there are some great offers available if you look hard enough. Choose a bed that will dominate the center of your room, but that will still give you room for a bedside table on both sides. A huge headboard is a great way to make your bed look amazing and stylish.

The mattress is also a key part of your bed, so invest as much as you can. Take the time to visit your local suppliers and try out the different options. Choose a supplier that guarantees you can return your mattress if it doesn't suit you without being penalized. Reputable mattress suppliers understand that it takes time to make sure a mattress is right for you. Remember that going to bed should feel like going home. The sensation of floating on a cloud while being cocooned in a warm ball of cotton wool may feel fanciful, but your bed should be the most important piece of furniture you have. Support from your mattress will help your posture and sleep, and you will function better after a nourishing night on a supportive base.

If you are planning to redecorate your room, choose some colors that will be restful and help you sleep. Neutral colors are perfect for the bedroom as they can complement almost any other color, so you can be more creative with your accessories. Blue is a calming choice of hue for your walls, which can be combined with lavender, green, or pink for a feminine effect.

White can be a perfect choice as it freshens up your space and is great if your budget is limited. Team white walls with warm shades like teal and brown for a modern look or stick with pastels for an inviting yet relaxing feel. Some people love gray in the bedroom, but it is important to keep the shades light as dark hues can be depressing and sad.

CHOOSE YOUR BEDDING CAREFULLY

When you choose your clothing, you tend to buy things that are a pleasure to wear and that make you feel comfortable. The same ideals should apply to bedding. The highest quality bedding you can afford should be your obvious choice. Try to look for high thread counts that will ensure your bedding is soft yet durable. Egyptian cotton is one of the best choices and will feel amazing against your skin.

Make sure your duvet is puffy and light, so you feel covered but not weighed down. Your duvet should feel like a cozy haven for you to snuggle down and cover-up. Some people swear by feather duvets, while others choose synthetic materials. Try out the feel of the duvet in-store and make sure you aren't allergic to any types of fillings. A top-quality naturally filled duvet can be an investment as it can last for up to 25 years if cared for properly. Check out some online resources for reviews and suggestions for your new cover, and make sure you choose wisely.

Once you have all the basics covered, it is now time to let your inner designer loose! Choose a furry faux throw to make your bed look special, and maybe jazz it up with some sparkly cushions. A Well-placed throw can turn the most mundane bed into space for a queen (or king!). Creating layers is a great way to make your bed look and feel inviting.

Remember that you can never have too many cushions and pillows! When you have these soft options on your bed, you can just sink in, cover yourself with the throw, and have a restful nap without messing up the covers! Genius!

CONSIDER WHAT FURNITURE SHOULD BE IN YOUR BEDROOM

If you are planning to retreat to your room during the day, you will need an extra option to relax in. Ground your room with a comfortable chair and table combination. If you have the option, place these next to the window so you can sit in peace and consider the beauty of nature as you sip on a herbal tea. This table will also provide the perfect place to put your favorite reading materials on or double up as a writing space. Make sure to have a notebook and pen handy to jot down your thoughts.

A large chest at the bottom of your bed can double up as a handy storage space. It can be used to keep your throws, bedding, and extra pillows in, as well as providing a seating alternative. Choose a solid wooden piece that looks classic and well-built as this will give your room a focal point that looks classic and dependable.

CHOOSE YOUR ARTWORK

Most people have different ideas about how art should be displayed in the bedroom. Some believe it is distracting, and the walls should be left bare of pictures or paintings that take your mind off sleep, while others believe it can be restful. If you do decide to make art part of your décor, consider some artwork you can do yourself. Landscapes and pastoral works look great and avoid some of modern art's busyness while keeping the atmosphere chilled.

Have you considered some alternative ways of decorating your walls? Tapestries and collages provide an alternate way to bring some color to your environment. Ask your kids or friends to create pieces they think you might like and bring a sense of love to your walls!

CURTAINS

Complete darkness can help us sleep deeply, and the only way to achieve this is with blackout blinds. Now, these may seem like something we needed in wartime and a bit OTT for today's furnishings but think again. Blackout blinds simply mean you are blocking all light sources from disturbing your slumber. They are extremely effective and can be a beautiful addition to any room.

Try these pretty and stylish options to make sure you get a good night's sleep:

1) Pottery Barn offers a Belgian flax option that comes in 8 different elegant colors and makes a stylish statement and is efficient at blocking out light.

2) Target offers Medallion blackout curtains for those shoppers who love a patterned option for their windows. For less than $40, your bedroom can look stylish and remain free from outside light.

3) Home Depot offers a Cellular shade curtain that not only blocks the light but also creates air chambers to insulate your room.

LIGHTING

Once you have made your room free from outside light sources, you will need to choose how to light your space. Relaxation and calm can be achieved by creating the perfect ambiance with your lighting choices. Your bedroom lighting can make or break your scheme. Imagine you have the most glorious bed surrounded by amazing accessories, yet your lighting is harsh and unflattering. Not good, right?

There are three types of lighting to consider when choosing your bedroom illumination options. These are ambient, accent, and task lighting. Ambient lighting makes the room seem as if it is lit with natural sunlight. Accent lighting can be used to pick out certain features within the room, while task lighting is used to help you read or do other stuff in the room.

The type of lighting you chose will depend on the size of your room. It can be as simple as a bedside lamp or fairy lights or as striking as led lighting around a mirror. You don't want to create clutter with multiple options in a small room, so you may want to consider a traditional central light with adjustable options to suit your mood. Dimmer switches will help you regulate the light intensity you require with just one light.

Wall-mounted lights are the perfect way to make your lighting look decorative as well as practical. Use the space you have to create a focal statement and offer a relaxed way to switch the focus by adjusting the light position.

Bedroom lighting doesn't always need fancy shades to create an impact. Bare bulbs can make white walls look like they have a beach theme when combined with coastal decorations but make sure you choose a low-wattage bulb for a less intense glow.

SMELL

We all know how comforting aromas can be. Coming home to the smell of baking bread or fresh coffee can make you feel like your house is giving you a hug, so why not take that idea into the bedroom? There are some fabulous linen sprays available that help you introduce relaxing smells into your bedroom. Linen sprays also make your bedding smell freshly laundered with just one spritz!

Here are some of the best options available

- The Laundress deodorizing spray gives your room and linen the 5-star treatment with just a quick spray. Smell sandalwood, jasmine, and lily of the valley undertones contained in this natural spray for just $16 a bottle.

- PF Candle Co. has a range of sprays to suit all occasions. One of the most popular is the Sandalwood and Rose option that gives your linen a woody smell without being overly floral.

- Positive Essence linen spray has lavender overtones and is one of Amazon's more inexpensive options. This restful no-nonsense spray can make your bedroom smell divine.

CHAPTER 6

PILLOWS

A Comprehensive Guide

The history of pillows can be traced back as far as the Mesopotamian civilization, which existed around 7000 BC. Since the beginning of time, humans have been looking to improve how they sleep, and today is no different.

Ancient Egyptians used stone pillows to elevate the heads of the dead as the human head was regarded as the most sacred part of the body. The use of these wooden or stone accessories also became part of the sleeping routine of the rich and famous. They believed that elevating the head improved blood circulation and kept the subject safe from evil forces.

The ancient Chinese people also used hard materials to create pillows, with porcelain being the most popular. They adorned these pillows with elaborate paintings of humans and animals in decorative and colorful forms.

The ancient Europeans began to realize the benefits of a softer filling for their pillows as they used them to kneel in the church, and the introduction of feathers and straw made them more comfortable for sleeping. These softer pillows were still only available to upper-class members, and commoners were left to sleep without elevated necks and heads.

In Medieval history, the story of the pillow took an unexpected turn. The fashion was to wear a pillow around the neck that supported the head and, when removed, could be used as a sleeping aid, but the monarch of the age, King Henry VII, took umbrage with the perception of the pillow. He stated that wearing pillows meant men were perceived as weak and forbade them for everyone except for pregnant women.

The current use of pillows is completely different as humans understand the need for comfort when they sleep. The choice of materials, size, filling, and features are immense. When it comes to choosing the right pillow for yourself, you need to know exactly what is available and what suits your needs.

MATCHING YOUR PILLOW TO YOUR SLEEP POSITION

Every night an average person sleeps at least 6-8 hours. Your head and neck spend hours every night on your pillow, which is why choosing the right size pillow is key to a healthy, pain-free neck. A pillow that doesn't support your head and neck properly can create tension in your neck muscles and cause neck pain.

 If your pillow is hurting your neck before sleep or causing neck pain/stiffness the next day, if you cannot find a comfortable position with your pillow or keep changing the pillow position under your neck and shoulders, then you need to carefully choose a good pillow. Pillows that adopt your natural cervical/neck curve and help your shoulder adjustment are the best to prevent neck pain and get comfortable quality sleep.

As a physiotherapist, I always recommend that it is essential to find your neutral spinal position, so your pillow should be chosen to keep your spine straight and your head and neck correctly supported. This will always help to prevent pressure on your neck muscles from the weight of your head throughout the night. This will not only help you to have a good quality sleep but will also prevent neck pain by reducing muscular spasm/tension. Most scientific studies suggest that using correct support/pillows also prevents wear and tear in neck vertebrates, and this always helps to prevent neck Osteoarthritis (Spondylosis). Depending on your sleep position and size of the body, as well as the angle between your neck and shoulder, your pillow may need to be thicker or thinner than your current choice to find this neutral position. If you are unsure what position you adopt for most of your sleep, ask your partner to watch you when you sleep.

Side Sleepers

- Your spine should be parallel to your mattress and align with it when you lie on your side.
- Your pillow (pillow material) must be thick enough for a good support of the base of your neck and must also support your head.
- If you suffer from neck pain, try a pillow that offers some smooth curve support to your shoulders as well as your neck.
- Thicker pillows with sizes between 10cm to 12 cm in loft thickness will often be the best choice for this position. Counter memory foam pillow with double adjustment of sizes i.e. one side is 12cm, and another size is 10 cm, so you can adjust accordingly.

Back Sleepers

- Align your spine with the mattress so that your neck is as stable as possible. Back sleepers can suffer from a twisted neck if your pillow is too thick or too thin.
- Choose a pillow that ensures your nose and chin are levels, so your head is at a premium position for sleeping.
- Choose a pillow that supports your shoulders and keeps the airways clear.
- Thinner pillows will often provide the best support, but please make sure that the size of the loft must not

be too thin to bend or dip your head backward and cause sleep disturbance or neck pain. I would recommend an adjustable loft pillow or Counter memory foam pillow with double adjustment of sizes i.e. one side is 12cm, and another size is 10 cm, so you can adjust accordingly

Stomach Sleep

- This sleep position is not common, as a physiotherapist, I will not recommend this positing and would suggest adopting as soon as possible either side sleeping or back sleeping position. The reason to avoid this position is there is no adoption of a cervical spine neutral position. When we sleep on our stomach, there is no breathing hole in the mattress, and naturally, we twist our neck to either side; this rotation of the neck causes tension in our neck muscles for hours during the night. This position is not only creating tension in our neck but also disturbs our lower back curve and alignment of our knees and legs, causing neck as well as lower back and knee pain.
- The best choice of pillow is a 10cm loft memory foam or adjustable loft standard thin pillow.
- Some people may find they sleep better in this position when they choose a thin pillow.

How To Choose A Pillow:

To achieve a comfortable sleep and avoid neck pain, we must ensure that our head, neck, and top of the cervical spine align and form a straight line. We must also ensure to sleep with a pillow that is neither too high nor too low to avoid neck pain and sleep depravations. Another important point we must need to consider that our pillow should not be too soft so our head sinks into neither it should be too firm to irritate our pressure points. As a physiotherapist, I will stress the point again that a pillow for neck and shoulder comfortable support must be firm enough to hold our head at an ergonomically correct angle, as well as soft enough to alleviate pressure points and promote quality sleep.

Ergonomically correct angled cervical orthopedic pillows are better suited to back sleepers, especially if they suffer from neck pain or arthritis of the neck. The best cervical pillows can change your life! They will help you sleep longer and manipulate your shoulder muscles as you sleep. The position of your spine helps any injuries heal and regenerate by alleviating pressure on it during the night. They also reduce snoring by keeping your airways at an optimal angle.

Many physiotherapists and other health care professionals recommend these types of pillows and will often know the best product for your particular needs. They come in many shapes and sizes and can alleviate many of the problems associated with improper sleep alignment. When neck pain occurs, it can lead to other symptoms, including:

- Headaches
- Shoulders and Neck pain
- Back pain
- Hip discomfort
- Spinal pain

These symptoms can then lead to anxiety and stress, which can prevent restful sleep and develop into more serious problems.

These pillows are an investment in your health, which is why the makers offer a return policy if the buyer isn't satisfied. Never choose an orthopedic or ergonomic pillow that doesn't offer this option. Trusted suppliers understand that your pillow is an essential part of a good night's sleep and prevents neck and back pain.

TYPES OF PILLOWS TO CONSIDER

Memory Foam Pillows

As the name suggests, these pillows utilize all the positive elements of the different foams and bring them together to make the ultimate memory foam pillow. They are great for people who want to experience the benefits of memory foam like cooling and molding but prefer to avoid the negative aspects like rigidity.

This type of pillow is becoming increasingly popular as they enhance the quality of sleep for the user. They are designed to mold to your neck and shoulder shape and adopt your natural curve.

Cooling Gel Memory Foam

These pillows appeal to people who suffer from high levels of body heat during the night. They have a special gel in the form that reduces heat retention and allows it to escape into the air. These pillows work better when covered with pillowcases that are moisture-wicking. These can be as natural as bamboo cases or as scientific as NASA engineered fabrics called Outlast. The choices are mainly dependent on the budget when it comes to cooling pillowcases.

Shredded Memory Foam (adjustable loft)

This filling is less rigid than standard memory foam as it has been shredded into smaller pieces. This makes it more moldable, and they feel more like a traditional pillow than rigid foam. They can be adapted to fit the sleeper's needs and provide them with a comfortable and breathable option for sleep.

Synthetic Down Pillows

The filling for these pillows is one of the most comfortable options available on the market. This gives a light and exceptionally soft base for sleep, which is both natural and breathable. The pillow's comfort depends on the quality of the fibers, and less expensive options can lose their shape. Even the top end synthetic pillows needs a great deal of fluff to keep their shape.

Polyester or synthetic pillows can be used as an alternatives for people who have allergies to down or feather. They are easier to maintain and cost a lot less than natural down pillows. They can be washed in the machine without losing their shape, and they can be as soft as cotton.

CARING FOR YOUR PILLOW

Sometimes it can be easy to forget just how much support and comfort we get from our pillows and that they need some love and care to keep them effective. Once you have chosen your pillow, you must look after it.

Before You Use It

Consider buying a protector for your pillow. They provide an extra layer of protection from natural substances like oils and bodily fluids that can stain your bedding. Most protectors are inexpensive and easily purchased from bedding suppliers.

Daily

Show your pillow some love! Give it a good shake and fluff to help it keep its shape. This will help kill any dust mites and other nasties that may have crept in, and it keeps your pillow fresh and clean.

Weekly

Check the instructions on your pillow's label and if it is suitable for washing, then put it on a gentle cycle every week to keep your pillow fresh and clean. Remember to use a softer detergent for washing your pillows as you don't want harsh chemicals to become trapped in the filling.

Modern pillows often come with best-before dates. These remind you that pillows are not for life and will need replacing at least every two years. Of course, some pillows are designed to last longer, but it is still recommended to do the pillow test every month just in case!

When you choose the correct pillow for your sleep, you are supplying a vital piece of kit for a good night's sleep. They can be the cornerstone of your sleeping experience and should be chosen with consideration.

A comfortable pillow can be as crucial as a well-fitting pair of shoes. We all know the agony of ill-fitting footwear, but our pillow can be just as disruptive if it isn't suitable for our needs. Nobody chooses to wear uncomfortable shoes, so why would we choose an uncomfortable pillow? To disturb your sleep or cause pain in your neck.

CHAPTER 7

SLEEPING POSITIONS

ow Posture Can Change the Quality of Your Sleep

How you sleep, and the position that you find most comfortable is a matter of personal choice. There are some benefits from certain poses that can help your breathing or ease any back pain. Some sleep experts tell us that sleeping on your side is the best way to get a decent night's sleep but are they right?

The truth is there is no one size fits all solution for getting quality sleep, but we can make better judgments when we know the benefits and risks associated with different ways of sleeping.

SLEEPING POSITIONS

How They Impact Your Body

Sleeping Baby or the Fetal Position

Who knew that over 40% of us revert to our childhoods when it comes to sleeping positions? This position is mainly lying on your side with an inward curl and bent legs, just like a baby in the womb. This helps to keep the spine aligned and the airways open. Sleeping like a baby also allows us to feel safe and warmer and makes us sleep deeply and uninterrupted. The position is not just a comfortable sleep posture, but it is also a natural way to relieve pain from lower back problems.

There are some downsides to the fetal position. If a sleeper adopts this pose while sleeping on their left side, it puts considerable pressure on the internal organs, including the liver, lungs, heart, and stomach. Sleepers should always choose the right side to avoid compression of these essential organs.

How to Train Your Body to Adopt to the Fetal Position

Place pillows around your body to arrange your limbs and legs into your chosen position. You may feel more comfortable if you have a cushion or pillow to clasp and raise your legs toward.

Sleeping on Your Side

Most people will choose this position for over 50% of their total sleep. If you sleep on the left side, this pose will help your body deal with heartburn and acid reflux. It also boosts your natural digestion process and deals with the harmful toxins that need to drain to your lymph nodes where they can be expelled. Your brain will benefit from this position as improved circulation means it will receive fresh blood to clean away waste and harmful elements.

Side sleepers will need to switch positions during the night as they might experience numbness in their arms due to sleeping for a long time on one side. Sleeping on your right side will once again put pressure on your vital organs and shouldn't be your preferred side. People with shoulder pain or other related injuries will find this posture uncomfortable, so they should choose a more comfortable position.

How to Train Your Body to Sleep on Your Side

Placing pillows along the spine can remind your body to return to this comfortable pose if it is tempted to change position, but this is one of the most natural sleep positions, and your body shouldn't need too much persuasion to adopt it. As a physiotherapist, I would like to recommend that for more comfort, always keep a pillow or a cushion between your legs or knee a comfortable posture.

Sleeping on Your Stomach

When you see pictures of cute babies asleep, they will often be in this type of pose. Cheek and stomach on the blanket and butt in the air, just like nature intended, right? Well, actually, this pose is good for stopping snoring, but that's about all.

Sleeping on your stomach is probably the closest you will come to a "bad" sleeping position. Your back is flattened and fails to achieve its natural curve while sleeping with your face turned to one side will put an unnatural strain on your neck. Aside from these drawbacks is the additional fact that the body is tempted to bring one leg up to form a stepping position when sleeping in this position. This can strain the hips and lower back area as well as the knees when the body is twisted and contorted during sleep.

How to Make the Situation Better if You Tend to Sleep in This Position

You can help recreate the spine's natural curve by placing a pillow under the abdomen and avoiding lower back pain. Neck strain can be reduced with a flatter pillow for the head, and a low memory foam option will help you sleep more naturally.

You can also keep one pillow each side of your face, while one under your forehead to make a breath hole for your face and avoid tension and twist in your neck. Keeping all theses suggestions in mind I will stll recommend to avoid this sleeping position and adopt side or back sleeping position for quality sleep and for the prevention of further neck and back pain.

Lying Flat on Your Back

Sometimes called the soldier position or sleeping on duty, this position is all about keeping your body level. This is a great position for people with spinal problems or injured limbs. The traditional pose is flat on the back with the arms tucked in to the side. If you are looking for a less uniform position, the knees can be slightly elevated, and arms can be folded across the chest.

This position is not recommended for people who suffer from acid reflux, heartburn, or sleep apnea. Some women prefer this position in the later stages of pregnancy as it is more comfortable and takes the pressure off their stomach. Sleeping on your back also disrupts your breathing as the tongue is in an unnatural position, and it disrupts natural breathing. The good news is this position does possess some cosmetic advantages as your face is free to breathe. As sleepers lie with their face toward the ceiling, gravity can perform wonders and discourage wrinkles!

How to Improve Your Position for Spine Alignment

Sleeping with a flattened pillow under the lower back will help keep the spine straight. Keeping a good adjustable pillow under the head will further increase the alignment of the back, while keeping a cushion or pillow under your knees will help you to achieve more comfortable spinal alignment.

Starfish

Unless you have a huge bed and a very forgiving partner, chances are you won't sleep in this snow angel pose! Around 5% of people regularly sleep in this position with their legs and arms splayed out like a starfish. Besides taking up a lot of space, this position has the same drawbacks as lying flat on your back, which leads to snoring and sleep apnea.

There is no obvious way to encourage your body to sleep in this pose, and it just seems to come naturally to some people.

Sleeping with Elevated Legs

Most successful athletes will tell you this is the best position to sleep in if you want to encourage blood flow and increased circulation. They often sleep like this following a hard game or workout as it helps to heal muscles and repair any damage to limbs. Sleeping like this reduces the pressure on the feet and calves and lets the blood flow freely around the body. This is healthy for both the body and the brain, just like improved circulation while sleeping is highly recommended.

There aren't many cons to this sleeping position when the elevation is at the right height. If the legs and feet are over elevated, it can cause damage to the blood flow and lead to numbness.

Sleeping While Sitting Up

Okay, we know this isn't part of the traditional sleeping poses associated with sleeping during the night, but most of us have fallen asleep in this position at one time or another, so we should know how it affects our body. The obvious benefit of this position is the ease of getting in and out of it, but it isn't recommended for prolonged sleep.

This sitting posture is perfect for power naps and is often used by people in demanding jobs with pressure on them to sleep whenever they can, but the position is not a natural sleep position and can make sleep less beneficial than more traditional positions. This type of sleep means that the body may be resting, but it isn't reaping the other benefits of sleep like healing and revitalizing.

When choosing a sleeping position, there are many factors to consider. Age, physical injury, sleep apnea, pregnancy, and snoring all need to be factored in. Physical and medical factors may suggest we need to change position, but it can be challenging to make such a major change to how we sleep. Using pillows and other supports will help, but we will often revert to what we know best.

How Does Your Sleeping Position Affect Your Choice Of Mattress?

When you are choosing the right mattress for your bed, it is important to consider how your sleeping position influences your choice.

Here are some suggestions for different sleep positions

1) Back Sleepers

These types of positions are all about protecting and supporting the spine. It is essential to provide the right amount of pressure for the small of the back and choosing the wrong firmness will cause more back-related health problems like stiffness and pain.

Back sleepers should choose a medium-firm mattress with around a 6-7 on the firmness scale. This should be topped with two inches of softer material known as a comfort layer to provide a layer of relaxation.

The perfect mattresses are latex, memory foam, and innerspring. The support and contouring provided by them alleviate back strain and gives a healthy level of support.

As a physiotherapist, I always recommend memory foam with innerspring as it can naturally adot your sleeping body positing and provide enough support with good comfort for quality sleep.

2) Side Sleepers

Side sleepers have more to think about than back sleepers as they have more bony parts of the body to contend with. Side sleepers should aim for a slightly softer mattress with a 5.5 to 6.5 range of firmness. Airbeds and memory foam mattresses can help the sleeper cushion their shoulders, hips, and knees. Side sleepers should consider a comfort layer of around 3" and work with that figure.

If there isn't a deep enough comfort layer, side sleepers will suffer from aches and pains and may even find their sleep is disturbed by discomfort.

For side sleeper I always recommend my client a mattress with softness as well as good support like memory foam or memory foam with innerspring.

3) Stomach Sleepers

These sleepers need to have soft types of mattresses. A range of firmness between 5 and 4.5 is best for this type of sleep. Soft mattress will help their body to adopt the natural position for comfort and quality sleep. If they are prone to staying in the same position during the night, they should consider just a single inch of the comfort layer. The hybrid type mattress can be a comfortable choice for stomach sleepers and can help reduce soreness and discomfort from this unconventional sleeping position.

Of course, most people are classed as combination sleepers who may fall asleep on their side and wake up on their back. Most people know the position they favor and should base the choice of a mattress on this knowledge.

How Your Weight Affects Your Choice Of Mattress?

Our body weight is another significant factor we need to consider when choosing a mattress. This factor affects how different people perceive the firmness of different mattresses and affects how they choose the firmness grade they require. The heavier the sleeper is, the thicker the comfort level should be. Sleepers who weigh 120lbs may feel like a mattress is a 7 on the firmness grade, while a person weighing over 200lbs will feel it is closer to a 5. Heavier sleepers should consider an innerspring mattress, also known as a hybrid mattress.

These are mattresses with combination of classic innerspring coils and springs and layers of foam or latex. Choosing an eco-friendly option with all-natural high-quality materials will not just support your back and joints but also give you a durable mattress that allows ease of movement during sleep.

There are many options available for innerspring mattresses depending on your budget, but we always recommend choosing the best quality option you can afford. Ideally, you will choose a high-end luxury mattress with high durability levels for a reasonable price. Choose a company that offers you a return policy that ensures you can try their product for an extended period. This should be at least 120 nights as your body need at least three months to adjust to a new mattress.

CHAPTER 8

HOW DOES FOOD IMPACT YOUR SLEEP?

After a lousy night's sleep, most people will point the finger at stress, their partners snoring, or noise pollution to find the cause, but it could be something as simple as a late-night snack that is stopping you from catching up on your sleep. Knowing what foods to eat before bedtime and which to avoid won't cure all your sleeping woes, but it can go a long way to helping you fall (and stay!) asleep.

Some foods will sap your energy and can trigger heartburn and other related conditions. If you find your sleep is disturbed by gastric symptoms, then it may be time to look at your nighttime diet and what foods you should be cutting out.

The good news is that not all foods are bad for your sleep, and some will positively impact your night's rest. Nobody is suggesting that eating these foods will cure your insomnia or guarantee a great night's sleep, but it will help! Check out the foods that are more likely to help you drop off and the foods that will ruin a good night's sleep faster than you can say "insomnia"!

FOODS THAT WILL HELP YOUR SLEEP

1) Chicken Noodle Soup: If you are looking for comfort food to send you off to dreamland, then this soup is ideal. It is easy to digest, comforting, and will give you a sense of relaxation before you go to bed. If you are choosing a shop-bought soup, pick one with low sodium content as too much salt can be bad for you. The perfect way to know exactly what is in your soup is to make your own.

2) Sweet Potato: These hearty veggies are a great bedtime snack providing they aren't served as French fries! They contain vitamin B6, which boosts your mood and encourages the body to produce melatonin, which helps you prepare for sleep. They are packed with fiber, which will stop you from waking up hungry during the night. Try spiralizing a sweet potato and coating the noodles with peanut sauce for a healthy bedtime snack.

3) White Rice: A single cup of white rice may seem a strange choice for a nighttime snack, but it can help you fall asleep quicker. The carbohydrates in rice promote feelings of fullness, which help you feel restful before bed. Rice is not the healthiest option, so make sure you limit your portion size and season with a splash of soy sauce.

4) Oily Fish: Salmon, tuna, mackerel, herring, and sardines are just a few options of oily fish that are high in Omega 3 and vitamin D. When consumed as a late-night snack, they produce serotonin that tells the body it's time to sleep. You have option of eating them as a stand-alone dish, or you can make them into a tasty snack like butter baked salmon or a tuna melt.

5) Cherries: If this fruit is your go-to option for snacking, you can benefit from the melatonin content in cherries and have a tasty snack before bed! If you prefer a drink, just one small drink of cherry juice will help you fall asleep successfully.

6) Low Sugar Cereal with Skim Milk: If the thought of having this breakfast option blows your mind, then read on! We all know warm milk is a sleep-indulgent option, but it is a snooze fest for your body when it is combined with cereal. The glycemic properties of cereal combine with the amino acid tryptophan to send the signal to your brain that it's time to hit the pillows.

7) Bananas: These amazing fruits contain the triple whammy of melatonin, serotonin, and tryptophan. Add to the mix potassium and magnesium, and it can be hard to find a reason not to eat these super fruits. The muscle-relaxing source of magnesium helps older people get more sleep by extending the time they spend sleeping in a bed rather than just lying there. Banana bread is a perfect choice to use these fruits to make a tasty snack that is easy to digest. Replace white flour with oat flour and swap out butter for Greek yogurt for a healthier option, which will keep the calorie count low!

8) Nuts: Another great source of magnesium is nuts! Peanuts, cashews, and almonds will give you the perfect tag team of calcium and tryptophan to make them one of the most sleep-inducing foods on the market. If you prefer a more traditional snack for your evenings, try blending coconut oil with a handful of nuts to make super healthy butter options. You can then top your tasty, healthy banana bread with crunchy nut butter to get a double dose of magnesium.

9) Turkey: If you love a meat option as a late-night snack, then choose lean turkey meat. Just 3 oz. of turkey can provide you with enough tryptophan to lengthen the hours you spend asleep. Try swapping out beef for ground turkey and begin to benefit from its sleep-inducing qualities. Meatballs, sloppy joes, and chili can all be made using this healthy lean meat that will be healthier without sacrificing taste. Turkey meatloaf is the perfect way to benefit from a slice of heaven before you go to bed!

10) Cottage Cheese: Before you dismiss this option because the idea of cottage cheese being boring, bland, and restricted to weight watching, just keep reading. It is rich in protein that will keep you feeling full during the night, and it also contains our old friend tryptophan! Blend it with salmon to make a nutritious dip or spread it on whole grain toast. Cottage cheese and turkey can also create a classic lasagna dish that is filling and healthy.

As with most foods, it is significantly important to leave a period before eating your snacks or meals and then retiring. The trick is to use the food to comfort your body and relax it without over-filling your stomach. The foods listed above will make sure your gastric juices won't interrupt your sleep, and you will feel full all night.

FOODS TO AVOID

Evenings are notoriously difficult when it comes to food. You are relaxing after a stressful day, and it can be tempting to think treating yourself is a great idea, but a little of what you fancy can be the reason you are tossing and turning during the night. Foods that cause acid reflux and other gastric complications should be avoided and replaced with the options above.

1) Ice Cream: Top of the list must be that awesome spoonful of your favorite Ben and Jerry ice cream that you crave right before hitting the sheets. It contains a high sugar level, which will boost your insulin levels and prevent you from sleeping soundly. Eating ice cream is often a classic response to stressful situations, so it may come as a surprise to find that this creamy delight actually increases cortisone levels. So, instead of soothing your mind, it floods it with stress hormones, which makes it virtually impossible to fall asleep. Replace your store-bought ice cream with whipped up frozen bananas for a tasty snack that looks and tastes like ice cream but will help you fall asleep.

2) Acidic Foods: The acid in foods like grapefruit or bacon will relax your sphincter, which then leads to acid reflux. This can cause heartburn and interrupt even the soundest sleep. Tomatoes are especially acidic, and any tomato-based product should be avoided after 2 p.m. to help promote a healthy slumber.

3) Cheeses: This dairy option is a bit of a curveball for sleep seekers. You can eat certain options like halloumi or goat cheese in the evenings without any repercussions, while aged cheese like Gouda can prove troubling. The difference is the acid in aged cheese is responsible for the production of norepinephrine, which will trigger your natural alertness and prevent restful sleep. Of course, if you have even a hint of dairy intolerance, you should cut out cheese altogether!

4) Chocolate: Another tricky one for insomniacs! While the tryptophan in milk chocolate can aid sleep, dark chocolate is another matter! Dark chocolate may seem a healthier option, but it contains caffeine, which we all know isn't great for sleep! Just an average portion contains the same hit of caffeine as a cup of coffee, so it should be ditched as a late-night option. Instead, have a smaller portion of milk chocolate or fudge to keep your sweet tooth satisfied.

5) Take Out Foods: How often have you finished a productive day or a pleasant night out with a portion of take-away food and lived to regret it? That's because your classic choices are loaded with fat and will keep your body up all night trying to process them. Hearty burgers, loaded nachos, and tasty pizzas will all interfere with your night's sleep and leave you feeling tired and restless in the morning.

6) Spicy Foods: We all know what certain spices do to our bodies. That hit of chili or splash of cayenne may make our foods taste great, but they also have a diverse effect on our core temperature. Even a small splash of Tabasco or any other spicy sauce will make your metabolism work overtime. This makes your body temperature rise and leads to feelings of alertness, which makes it difficult to fall asleep.

7) Pasta Dishes: Pasta is filled with simple carbohydrates, which are prone to reduce serotonin levels. While it may make you feel full and initially feel tired, it will keep your body busy digesting it, interrupting your sleep. Now consider the sauces you serve with pasta. We already know that tomato-based products will cause problems, and when you add aged cheese to the mix, you have a smorgasbord of sleep deprivation. Skip the tomato-based pasta meals and replace them with lean meat options instead.

8) Raw Onions: Not only will you find it difficult to find someone to kiss, but you will also be kept awake if you snack on these seemingly healthy ingredients. A simple salad can be made super tasty with a handful of onions, but they will cause gas!

9) Steak Dinners: Those of us that love a steak know how much protein a good steak contains. This is great if you eat it earlier in the day but can be problematic in the evenings. The protein will remain in your body, and the digestion process will interrupt your slumber. If you want to eat a hearty meal, combine lean meats like turkey or chicken with green vegetables for your last meal.

10) Too Much Food: While this is not strictly a food type, it is probably the best advice you can take from this list. Some people love to go to bed completely stuffed, but it really won't help you sleep. It is important to make sure the food you eat is digested before you go to bed, and your body will thank you for it. It is important to point out that going to bed starving can be just as unhealthy and can lead to your body relying on your muscle and fat storage to feed itself.

The bottom line is to be sensible. Eat healthily and be informed about your choices, and your sleep will improve. Try keeping the unhealthy options out of your kitchen to avoid temptation and replace them with sleep-friendly foods. It will not only help your sleep improve but so will your overall health.

CHAPTER 9

CREATE THE PERFECT EVENING ROUTINE

to Improve Your Sleep

How do you typically spend your evenings? Do you always or sometimes bring work home with you or make yourself available for work-related contact? Are you faced with a mountain of chores or childcare? So, when do you relax, and what do you do to unwind? You may feel that winding down or quiet time spent relaxing is wasted, and you would rather be productive for as long as you can, but this can lead to problems.

If you are having problems sleeping because your mind is still in active mode, then it's time to rethink your evening routine. Choosing what to do in your "me time" is ultimately up to you, but here are some interesting things that could become part of your new routine.

HOW DOES A BEDTIME ROUTINE HELP?

- Focusing on sleep helps your mind and body prepare for it. When sleep is expected, it is easier to achieve.

- You can plan for tomorrow before going to bed as this stops you from worrying and overthinking things before you fall asleep.

- Following a fixed routine is like training for your mind.

- Most people don't realize how over-stimulating their normal activities are, and they don't understand how this impacts their sleep.

- Routines help you prioritize sleep.

- During your bedtime routine you can slow the flow of blood to your brain by thinking pleasant thoughts. Just imagine and close your eyes and you are on the beach, the warm sun licking your skin and the sound of the waves are sending you to sleep.

- Imagine you are in the arms of people you love. Feel the gentle pressure of their embrace as you fall asleep and feel comfortable and protected. You can buy weighted blankets that give the impression of being held if you prefer to sleep alone.

- Have a warm bath before you go to bed and use the time to dispel negative thoughts from your mind. Calming music and candles help you feel more relaxed and detached from your days' routine. This will take practice as we are conditioned to take our woes with us when we go to bed. We think that overthinking something will mean we solve it quicker, it doesn't, in fact overthinking makes it more difficult to reach solutions.

- Journaling can help you list the points of the day that need to be recorded. Create a positive account of what you have achieved that day and you can then sleep easier knowing you have been productive. Make a note of stuff you need to sort out the next day and then leave them in the journal rather than taking them to bed.

Your life circumstances will ultimately dictate the amount of time you can dedicate to your evening routine. Some people will be able to concentrate on it the minute they walk through the door, and others will only have around 30 minutes to dedicate to relaxing. Whatever the case, here are some great ideas to help you unwind.

FOOD AND DRINK

1) Stop Taking Caffeine Your Bedtime (At least Six Hours Before Bedtime)

Caffeine is a source of energy, and as such, it can inhibit your sleep. We have a natural sleep-inducing neurotransmitter called adenosine in our system that helps us fall asleep. Caffeine blocks our body's supply of adenosine and tricks it into believing we don't need sleep, and keeps us alert and awake when we should be resting. We all know and aware of the fact that coffee has caffeine in it, but some other common foods contain caffeine, which should be avoided. Protein bars, ice cream, some Greek yogurt, and energy drinks should not be eaten at least six hours before bed.

2) Have Your Evening Meal at Least Three Hours Before Bedtime

We have covered the types of food that help us go to sleep in another chapter, so we know what to eat, but even the best foods for sleep can cause problems if they are eaten just before bedtime. Having dinner at least two to three hours before sleep lets you digest your food completely and takes the stress off your stomach. Sleep comes easier to a fully relaxed body, and when your stomach is relaxed, this is a huge plus for relaxation.

3) Stop Water Consumption at Least Two Hours Before Sleep

How many of you have a bottle of water on your nightstand or bedside table at night? It was once believed that hydrating during the night was a healthy thing to do, but the fact is it just promotes bathroom visits during the night. Take the stress off your bladder and have your last drink of water early in the evening. You will have the chance to drink a restful cup of tea before you go to bed, so you won't be thirsty.

4) Switch Off Your Electronic Devices

Nobody is trying to be the technology police and insisting you strip back all your devices just because it's time to go to sleep. You may find it relaxing to watch cute cat videos on YouTube or play simple games on your hand-held console and if it works for you, then fine, go ahead. However, if you have problems falling asleep and have a lot of screen time during the evening, consider the science behind the reasoning.

Melatonin is essential for sleep, but it is sorely affected by exposure to bright or blue light. Two hours before your regular bedtime, the pineal gland will begin to release melatonin hormones to prepare you for sleep, and if you are busy on your devices, then it won't be effective. Try turning them off two hours before you go to sleep and see what happens to your sleep.

5) Meditation

When questioned about what stops them from going to sleep, people often reply that an overactive mind or stress combined with worry is the main reason they find sleep difficult. If this is true for you, then try a simple meditation routine before bedtime to clear your mind and prepare it for sleep.

A SIMPLE MEDITATION ROUTINE TO HELP YOU RELAX

- Find a comfortable spot on the floor and sit or lie down depending on which position is more comfortable.

- Take five conscious breaths, in through the mouth and out through the nose.

- Picture the three things in the world that you are most grateful for. These can be material things, family, your partner, or just items from nature as this exercise is all about elevating your mood.

- Draw a line under the day. Say thank you for your successes and forgive your mistakes. Tomorrow is a new day, and you want to start it with a clean slate. Forgive other people as well as this is the time to put negativity in the past.

- Now, take more mindful breaths and follow them as they leave your body. This process helps you to detach from your busy mind and become more relaxed.

6) Read

Unwinding before bedtime can be a challenge and some books are perfect for dealing with insomnia. Others can be too stimulating or irritating for nighttime consumption, so choosing the right book is essential.

Here are Some Soothing Reading Suggestions to Lull You to Sleep

• **"What We Talk About When We Talk About Love" by Raymond Carver**: This collection of short stories is perfect for romantics. It has 17 short stories focused on a group of friends and their experiences of love. The nature of this book makes it perfect for a quick read before you go to bed that will fill you with optimism and love.

• **"Just Listen" by Sarah Dessen:** This is a beautifully written novel based on the central character named Annabel. She is a musician who is passionate about her craft, and she will immerse you in her life and let you set your thoughts aside and escape the real world.

• **"I'll Give You the Sun" by Jandy Nelson**: This is a story all about family and how they can be there for you when you feel completely alone. This enlightening book will remind you that some people are destined to be in your life, and you should stop fighting the fact and let them in!

Of course, there are plenty of books you can read before bedtime, so the choice is yours. Try reading in your living room with a lamp, a throw, and no disturbances as you have your evening drink. This will help you relax and prepare for bed. Some people prefer to read in bed, and that's okay but not ideal. Remember the bedroom is just for sleep and intimacy!

7) Prepare a List of Reminders and Potential Worries for the Next Day

If you find it difficult to switch off and go to sleep because you are thinking about important tasks you need to do tomorrow, then try this simple exercise. Turn your mental to-do list into an actual to-do list. Are there any birthdays coming up that you need to buy a card or present for? Does the dog need to go to the vet, or is the car ready for an oil change? Stop the thoughts buzzing around your head and put them on paper instead.

8) Have an Evening Shower or Bath an Hour Before You Go to Bed

Experts recommend raising the body's temperature an hour before bed to signal the need to prepare for sleep. A warm bath with plenty of bubbles and a couple of candles will help you feel pampered, relaxed, and get you ready for a great night's sleep. Bath salts can also help you relax, but they don't come with bubbles!

9) Make Sure Your Bedroom is at the Optimum Temperature for Sleep

60 to 67 degrees Fahrenheit is thought to be the perfect temperature for sleeping, so make sure your bedroom is within this range. This will happen naturally in winter, but if the air temperature is above, you need to lower it.

Try the following methods of lowering bedroom temperatures:

• Open windows to create a natural draught and release hot, stuffy air.

• Install air conditioning or use a fan to cool the air.

• Use a cooling mattress pad.

• Use bedding that is light and allows circulation around your body.

10) Drink a Relaxing Evening Drink

Here are some sleep-inducing drinks that are perfect to have before you go to bed:

• **Chamomile Tea**: Made from a daisy-like flower, this type of tea has been used as a nighttime sleep aid for generations. It has many health benefits and is used to relieve cold symptoms, reduce anxiety, and improve skin health. Take 4 tbsp of dried chamomile leave and let them brew in a cup of hot water for 5 minutes before you consume the tea. If you want to sweeten your drink, use a tsp. of natural honey.

• **Warm Milk:** Some people regard warm milk as an old-fashioned bedtime drink that has no benefits regarding sleep quality. It may have been around for ages, but milk is actually a great source of tryptophan that produces serotonin, which increases melatonin levels. This promotes sleep and helps combat any other sleep disorders.

• **Golden Milk:** If warm milk is a bit bland and you fancy a more flavorsome nighttime tipple, then add some turmeric, ginger, and honey to your milk. Each of these ingredients contains compounds that help promote sleep, so when they are taken together, they are more effective and tastier!

• **Decaffeinated Green Tea:** Standard green tea has caffeine, so it should be avoided, but it also contains some soothing properties. Consuming a cup of decaffeinated green tea will help the brain relax and prepare for sleep. A study by the MDPI in 2017 showed the levels of amino acid in the beverage helped reduce stress levels and improved the quality of sleep in middle-aged individuals.

• **Almond Milk:** Almonds contain the hormone melatonin and high levels of tryptophan, which aid sleep, but they also contain magnesium. It has a pleasant nutty flavor and is available at most supermarkets and shops. Almond milk is a great alternative for people with allergies and those who are dairy intolerant. The magnesium element will help the body follow its natural sleep/wake cycle and improve sleep quality.

The bottom line is your routine should be achievable and comfortable. If you create a routine packed with must-do activities, you are just placing additional stress on yourself. Pick and choose what suits your lifestyle and your preferences. If reading isn't your preferred way to relax, try listening to music instead. Too many of us rely on the television or online entertainment to relax and then wonder why our brains are so overloaded when we go to bed.

What do you think is more relaxing, the image of Negan and Lucille from the Walking Dead or the relaxing sound of a gentle ballad before you drift off? It may seem obvious when we put it like that, but it is a fact that watching television or playing Call of Duty before bedtime is not considered relaxing!

CHAPTER 10

YOGA AND SLEEP

When you have insomnia, it can be frustrating to hear people recommending exercise before bed to help you sleep. If you aren't particularly flexible or athletic, you may feel that evening exercise is beyond your personal remit. Yoga can be a game-changer for improved sleep. Provided you use the right positions and postures, it can help exercise your body and relax your mind, helping you fall asleep quicker.

Another great reason to choose yoga as a nighttime activity is the fact that it can be performed almost anywhere and with extraordinarily little equipment. However, the stuff you do need can change the experience and make it safer and more comfortable.

The good news is choice is abundant when it comes to choosing yoga accessories, so it is essential to choose exactly what is right for you.

Here are some options for complete beginners who have no idea what to wear and what equipment to choose from:

WHAT TO WEAR
FOR YOGA

The first thing to do is dispel the idea that everyone who does yoga needs to look like a lycra-clad supermodel. Yoga is not about fashion and looking good on camera, despite what social media seems to suggest. The choice is yours and the outfits you choose can be snug, or they can be loose-fitting. However, baggy clothes can get in the way of your movements and prove dangerous.

You need to feel comfortable and supported as you begin your yoga session, so choose the clothes that make you feel great. If you prefer cotton tee-shirts to fitted Lycra shirts with built-in support, then go for it! If you want to spend upwards of $100 on fancy leggings and workout gear, there are plenty of quality items available.

YOGA MATS

There are so many options available for different budgets and the choices can feel overwhelming. Ask online for advice about what type of mat will suit you best, and then go to a sports outlet and inspect the mats you are considering.

Here are some of the considerations when buying a yoga mat:

- **Thickness:** Thicker mats are designed for practitioners with joint issues. If you need support when you practice, then check any stores that offer restorative mats that are 1/4" or even thicker. If you plan to be a traveling yoga practitioner, then you should choose a mat that is easy to pack and transport. These are generally around 1/16th of an inch and are listed as travel mats. Standard mats are somewhere in between and normal, around 1/8th of an inch thick.

- **Length:** Most mats come in a standard length that suits most people but if you are taller than average, choose a longer length mat. Most brands make the standard option of 5' 8" as well as the long option that is 6' 2".

- **Grip:** If you are transitioning from one position to another, your mat must stay still! Choose an option that is both grippy on the underside and has traction on the upper side. Your hands will get sweaty at some point, and your mat needs to cope with the slippiness and keep your hands and feet steady.

- **Material:** As with most products, mats are available in both eco-friendly options and other less eco-friendly materials. Check what the mat is made from and avoid flame retardant or off-gas options as they can have some negative side effects. Factor in your personal choices when choosing your mat and find what suits your needs without compromising your environmental conscience.

• **Price:** This is a no-brainer when it comes to choosing your yoga mat. If you aren't sure if this type of activity is for you, then you can get a suitable mat for less than $20. It will last you long enough for you to decide if you want to carry on and invest in your equipment later, but it will break down fairly quickly. If you decide to go for a top-end mat, you can spend around $100 or more, but your mat will last much longer.

Remember to shop around when choosing your mat. Sometimes stores will have an end of line discounts that can halve the price of your chosen mat, and we all love a bargain!

YOGA POSES FOR SLEEP

1) Bridge Pose, Also Known as Setu Bandhasana: This is a gentle stretching pose that will alleviate stress and provide a counterbalanced activity for people who spend all day at a desk or seated while operating a device. It will help your breathing become more even and shallow as the pose opens your chest for healthier access to your lungs.

How to Get into the Bridge Pose

- Lie on your back with your soles on the floor and knees slightly bent

- Place your arms alongside your body with your palms flat on the floor

- Maneuver your feet towards your hips with a slow walking movement

- Pull in your stomach until you feel pressure along your arms and a grounding sensation in your feet.

- Elevate your torso and breathe deeply for 20 seconds

- Lower your body to the floor and repeat

2) Lying Butterfly Pose, Also Known as Badhakonasana: This pose is a must-do pose for beginners and works wonders on the lower body. It stretches the inner thighs, groin, and knees while strengthening the back and hips. The butterfly pose improves bowel and intestine health and promotes relief from urinary discomfort.

How to Do the Butterfly Pose

- Sit down on your mat with a straight back

- Bring the soles of your feet together and move them toward your pelvis

- Grasp your feet with the corresponding hand and draw them closer to your body

- Breathe in deeply, and as you release the breath, place pressure on your knees and thighs to center them to the floor

- Repeats ten times

- Now begin the butterfly process with your legs. Simulate the butterfly wing action by flapping your legs while breathing normally

- Fly as high as you can with your newfound wings. The speed and intensity are your choices, and you can go as far as you feel comfortable with

- Slow down your flapping and stop the motion as you control your breathing

- Now lift your chin and your spine straight as you place your elbows on your knees

- Place pressure on your lower body and feel the benefit as you relax your muscles and control your breathing

- Raise yourself to a sitting position and gently release your grasp

- Straighten your legs out and shake them slowly before you relax and rise

3) The Dolphin Pose: This pose is classed as an inversion pose. Some inversion poses can be used to stimulate the body and increase energy levels, while simple ones are designed to do the opposite. As the name suggests, inversions place the body upside down. This encourages the central nervous system to wind down as we are signaling our feelings of safety with this typically vulnerable position.

Most of us have heard of the downward dog facing pose but realize it can pressure the wrists and is not suitable for everyone. A dolphin pose is a form of downward dog that is less damaging but can offer all the benefits of the more complex form of inversion.

It can help you find relief from stress and anxiety as well as asthma and menstrual pain. The pose helps strengthen the back while improving memory and concentration.

How to Do the Dolphin Pose

• Begin the pose on your mat with your hands and knees flat. Your wrists should be directly below your shoulders while your knees should be aligned to your hips. Splay your fingers and make sure your middle finger is pointing forward.

• Lower the elbows to the mat and raise your body onto your toes. Elevate your pelvis upward while keeping your bodyweight even. Bend your knees and feel how your shoulders and spine begin to feel the pressure.

• Now, straighten your legs as your body and legs form a classic triangular shape with your butt as the apex. You may feel the desire to walk your feet closer to your head but resist that feeling! Keep your body consistent and manipulate your shoulder blades and tailbone to stretch your body while widening your collarbone.

• Relax your head but keep it concentrated on your torso rather than letting it droop.

• Hold this pose as long as it's comfortable

• Exhale your breath and gently return your body to a relaxing position on the map

4) Savasana: This is a classic pose where yoga and sleep really begin to form a bond. To onlookers, savasana can just look like lying down and having a rest, but in reality, it is a form of meditation that prepares your body and mind for a good night's sleep. The restful posture will also help you reduce hypertension and calm anxiety and stress.

How to Do the Savasana Yoga Pose

- Lie on your yoga mat with the feet flat. Raise your knees and begin to move your feet past your hips so they are wider than your core. Now bring the knees together, so they support each other above the mat.

- Place your arms alongside your body with your palms turned up to the ceiling

- Close your eyes and be conscious of your breathing. Take note of every single breath as you inhale and exhale.

- Repeat a mantra that suits your peaceful place. This can be as simple as repeating "inhale" and "exhale" as you perform the action or as personalized as you like. If your main objective is to improve your sleep, then vocalize the fact! "I love to sleep, and I am going to sleep for seven hours tonight" may work for you while a more generalized soft mantra of love and peace can be repeated.

- Continue the process until you feel ready for your bed! Try not to fall asleep on your mat. Remember the idea is to get off your mat and into your comfortable bed!

BREATHING EXERCISES TO ENHANCE YOUR YOGA POSES

Sometimes it can be difficult to relax, and the yoga poses can be uncomfortable to achieve. If this happens, try these simple breathing techniques to help you get in the right frame of mind.

Effective Breathing Techniques

1) The 4-7-8 Technique

- Sit comfortably on your yoga mat

- Part your lips

- Breathe out completely and voice the action with a sound like a loud sigh

- Now, press your lips together and breathe in through the nose for 4 seconds.

- Hold this breath for 7 seconds

- Breathe out again with vigor making the appropriate sound for a full 8 seconds.

- Repeat four times to form a cycle

2) Alternate Nostril Breathing

- Sit on your mat with your legs crossed

- Place your left palm on your corresponding knee and then

close the alternate nostril with the corresponding thumb

• Exhale fully with the open nostril and then open the formerly closed nostril

• Continue the rotation until the nostrils feel wider and your stress levels have dropped.

3) The Papworth Method

This method is designed to deal with habitual yawning or sighing before sleep. It focuses on the abdomen and helps you breathe naturally.

• Sit with a straight spine on your mat or in bed

• Breathe in through your mouth for a full count of four

• Exhale through your nose for a full count of four

• Watch what happens to your abdomen as you breathe and listen for the sounds your body makes

The takeaway must be that when you are preparing to fall asleep, it is important to relax, shake off the stresses of the day, and prepare yourself for sleep. Combining yoga and breathing exercises into your nightly routine will help, but you must choose the poses and exercises that make you feel happy. If you push yourself too hard or injure yourself, then this pleasant therapy will become a chore.

Relaxation can be challenging, but it should never be unpleasant. Choose to challenge yourself with more complex yoga positions but make sure they are good for nighttime practices. Some yoga poses should only be done during the daytime as they can be exhilarating and increase energy levels.

CHAPTER 11

SLEEP THERAPY

Why is Therapy Better than Medication?

When you are deprived of sleep and desperate to catch up, it can be tempting to turn to medication to help. Some of these medications don't require a prescription and can be purchased in your local drug store, so why should you seek therapy?

Medication is fine for short-term sleeping issues like traveling across time zones or sleep loss following a medical procedure, but it can become addictive when used to treat sleeping disorders. Therapy will help you identify the reasons behind your disorder. It will allow you to change your behavior and thoughts to cure your disorder and develop healthy sleeping patterns for the future.

This doesn't mean that effective medication combined with therapy can't be used to treat sleep disorders, but the long-term goal is to create healthy lifestyle changes to enhance your sleep.

COGNITIVE BEHAVIOR THERAPY

The most widely used therapy to treat sleep disorders is CBT, cognitive behavior therapy. How the therapy is used depends on the individual and their specific needs. Some people benefit from individual sessions with a therapist, while others prefer group sessions. The length of therapy will also vary, but it is exceedingly rare that it will be an immediate or simple cure. Most therapists recommend that an effective CBT program should last between 5 to 8 weeks with one session per week. After this, the patient should see a marked improvement in their sleep patterns.

How Does CBT Work?

Understanding how CBT works is straightforward and involves two main components.

Cognitive Therapy: the therapist works with the patient to uncover the beliefs and cognitions that affect how they sleep. They will help discover what negative thoughts prevent sleep and how to change them.

Behavioral Therapy: the therapist will identify negative actions and habits that contribute to sleep deprivation and how to replace them with healthy behaviors and habits.

Initially, the patient will be asked to keep a sleep diary to decide which treatment will be most effective. This will include questions about your daily routine and sleeping patterns. Below is a standard sleep diary that you can fill in and take to the therapist to identify your particular problems.

STANDARD SLEEP DIARY

Fill in the sections daily before you go to bed.

Exercise: What did you do? What time of day was it? How long did you exercise?

Naps: Did you nap at all? When? Where? How long did you nap for?

Stimulants: Did you drink alcohol or coffee today? How many times? What type? When?

Emotions: Did you experience any intense feelings today? What? How intense? Cause?

Food and Drink: What did you eat and drink? When? How much?

Medications for Sleep: What did you take? When? Was it effective?

Pre-Sleep Meditation: Did you do any? How long?

Bedtime: What time did you go to sleep?

Wake Up Time: What time did you wake up?

How long did you spend in bed without sleeping?

Was your sleep interrupted? What did you do? How long was the break?

Quality and Depth of Sleep: Comment on your sleep quality.

Total Sleep Hours: How many hours of sleep did you get?

CHALLENGING THOUGHT PATTERNS IN CBT

This process is how the therapist will identify negative thoughts or cognitions and restructure them into positive and healthy affirmations that will change how patients perceive their thoughts.

Negative thoughts are part of deep-rooted reasons for sleep disorders and need to be dealt with. They can fall into different categories, and the therapist will identify and replace them with positive responses.

UNREALISTIC ASSUMPTIONS

Negative Thought: Everybody else sleeps well, so I should be able to. I want to be a normal, functioning person.

Sleep Assisting Thought: I am not alone with my problems. Lots of people suffer from insomnia or sleep deprivation. If I practice my new techniques, I will become better at falling asleep and staying asleep with time.

Overdramatizing Statements

Negative Thought: Tonight will be just another night of sleeplessness, and I will be awake for hours.

Sleep Assisting Thought: Every night is different. Tonight may be the night I get a good night's sleep.

Magnifying Negativity

Negative Thought: If I don't get enough sleep tonight, I will be sluggish at work. I may underperform and lose my job.

Sleep Assisting Thought: I am great at my job even if I am tired. I'm confident I can still get stuff done. The main aim is to get some rest and stop worrying about sleep.

Desperation

Negative Thought: Nothing will help me. I am at the end of my rope and beyond hope.

Sleep Assisting Thought: My sleep disorder is common, and many people have been cured. I am going to beat this disorder and benefit from great sleep in the future. I just need to stop worrying and focus on my positivity.

Prophesizing

Negative Thought: I won't fall asleep until past midnight. I know in my heart that I will be awake until the early hours of the morning.

Sleep Assisting Thought: Obviously, I don't know what will happen tonight. I hope my therapy session will help me fall asleep quickly and have a sound night's slumber.

Behavioral Techniques Used By Cbt Therapists To Improve Sleep Patterns

There are many techniques available in CBT, and therapists will be able to employ them depending on the individual symptoms a patient suffers from.

They can include the following strategies:

SRT (Sleep Restriction Therapy): Patients who have insomnia will often be encouraged to employ this strategy. They will work on eliminating naps and staying up past their normal bedtime. This form of sleep deprivation may seem harsh, but it ensures the patient goes to bed tired and ready for sleep. As time passes, it reinforces the positive association between bed and sleep.

Stimulus Elimination Therapy: Therapists use this technique to strip back the bedroom to its original form. As we discuss in other parts of this book, this means using a bedroom solely for sex and sleeping. The therapist will encourage the patient to take all external stimulants from their bedroom, including televisions and other electrical devices.

Removing Contradicting Intentions: The vicious circle of worrying about sleep and then suffering from bad sleep due to anxiety needs to be broken. The therapist will work with the patient to help them let go of the worrying, which will, in turn, help them sleep.

Biofeedback: The better we know our own bodies, the more control we can have over our sleep patterns. This type of therapy measures heart rate, muscular tension, and heavy breathing to identify when the body is in a state of anxiety that will stop you from falling asleep. Once you understand what is happening, you can take steps to lower the anxiety that impacts sleep patterns.

Hypnosis: Hypnotherapists use this strategy to place the patient in a deep state of relaxation before treatment. They will then work on changing any negative habits or cognitions to help promote effective sleep.

Therapists will also help with healthy lifestyle choices and other ways to improve your sleep. The key to success is to choose a therapist you can work with. They should be receptive to your questions and be someone you can talk to comfortably. You may be discouraged at the rate of recovery, but it is important to see the treatment through. You will see the benefits eventually.

Other Therapies That May Help You Improve Your Sleep

Polyphasic Sleep Therapy: Experts in this type of therapy believe that humans aren't meant to get all their sleep in one big chunk. They advocate dividing up sleep phases into gaps between tasks, for instance, spending three hours working from 7 a.m. until 10 a.m. and then going back to bed for two hours. While it works for some people, it can be quite difficult to maintain for long periods.

Acupuncture: This type of treatment involves stimulating various points of the body with needles to promote wellness. The opinion is divided as to the success of acupuncture as a treatment for sleep disorders, but there has been evidence that it can be used to spike melatonin levels. This can be used to treat sleep disorders related to menopause or problems following a stroke.

Phototherapy or Light Therapy: Primarily used to treat insomnia, this type of therapy can be used with the help of a medical form of light, or you can try a home-based method.

USING PHOTOTHERAPY AT HOME

1) Ensure Your Bedroom is Completely Dark: This may involve blinds or shades to block out any exterior sources of light and if you can still see light, use eye masks to block it out.

2) Flashlights or Night Lights: When you get up during the night, use a flashlight or a night light to light your way to the bathroom. Avoid putting on any mains lighting and reduce your exposure to artificial light.

3) Flood Your Bedroom with Light in the Morning: If you can use natural sunlight to do this, then that's great, but if you can't, try light-emitting alarm clocks. These range from 100 lux to 300 lux models and will flood your room with "sunlight" for up to 30 minutes in the morning. This type of alarm will improve how you feel when you wake up and help your circadian rhythms improve. They help you wake feeling refreshed and relaxed with a natural start to your day.

4) Bright Light Therapy: This involves using lightboxes to replace natural light during treatment. The lightbox has several tubes that produce bright light and is placed in a room on top of a table. The box will be activated for up to two or three hours, depending on the intensity of the light. Some boxes are between 3,000 lux and 5,000 lux and are available for around $200. More modern versions are safer and available with 10,000 lux lights so sessions can be reduced to less than an hour. These can cost as much as $500 but are safer because they protect the user from harmful UV rays.

There are light boxes available in different forms to fit into the environment. For instance, they are fashioned to look like desk lamps for an office setting or a visor for portable use.

The amount of time or number of sessions needed is dependent on the individual's needs and should be monitored carefully. Bright light therapy is highly effective but can involve some minor side effects if used improperly. Users can experience eye damage or headaches if overexposed to bright lights, so it is essential to follow the instructions that accompany your chosen box.

POPULAR LIGHTBOXES FOR LESS THAN $40

Philips Light Therapy Lamp

This lamp is fully interactable with your smartphone and can be used in the bedroom and living room. It will monitor the temperature and humidity of its environment and adjust the glow to sync correctly.

Miroco Light Therapy Lamp

This freestanding lamp is perfect for all users. It can be carried around and used at work as well as in the home and is fully customizable for morning and evening use.

Verilux Happy Light Portable Box

This is a low-cost option with a powerful lamp. The 10,000-lux lamp is one of the brightest on the market and is fully portable. It lacks some of the functions other lamps have but is simple to use and gives you a powerful source of light whenever you need it.

POPULAR LIGHTBOX FOR OVER $125

Hatch Restore Smart Light

If you fancy a more stylish light with preloaded sleep functions and wake up routines that look really cool, then you need to splash the cash! You can program this light to project different colors (22 of them!) as it brings the light back into your life!

CHAPTER 12

HOW TO TREAT SLEEP DISORDERS WITHOUT USING MEDICATION

When considering how to deal with sleep problems, it can be too easy to reach for medication to send us off into dreamland, but is that really the best solution? Medication can provide a short-term solution, but it fails to address the underlying causes that could be affecting how we sleep.

We have already discussed therapy and the important role it can play in treating sleep disorders, but what happens if therapy isn't for you? Can you seek help from other methods, or are you destined to suffer from poor sleep for the rest of your life? The good news is that medication and therapy are just two of the many solutions to treat sleep disorders, and you can choose from natural remedies or go full-on nerd and see what the tech world has to offer.

Let's see what the tech world holds for people who want to improve their sleep.

Consider how the world has changed in the last fifty years. What is the most significant change in your home? Chances are it is the number of gadgets and electronic devices. We all know that bad sleep can be caused by overexposure to these types of devices, so surely the tech world is an enemy when it comes to quality shut eye?

Quite the opposite, really, when it comes to ideas for improving sleep, then the most innovative ideas can be found in the world of tech.

REVOLUTIONARY WAYS TO GET GREAT SLEEP

1) Smart Pajamas: What do you imagine to be the best material for pajamas? Cotton or flannel, perhaps with a soft, comforting feel that is synonymous with winter. Think again. According to UnderArmour.com, the perfect material for pajamas is bio-ceramic fabric. This revolutionary fabric is made from over 20 different types of ceramic combined with polypropylene fibers to make sheets of fabric used to produce clothing items, like pajamas.

The fabric allows the wearer to benefit from:

- Increased circulation levels
- Higher levels of blood oxygen
- Significantly increased levels of muscle repair
- Tissue regeneration
- Pain relief
- Increased performance levels

According to the science behind this fabric, bio-ceramic textiles are designed to work with the body's natural healing qualities and harness the body's thermal energy. These amazing nightwear items may sound like something from the future, but they are available now for less than $100.

2) Smart Aromas: We know how beneficial aromas can be to change our mood and the power of a scented candle is special. However, the bedroom is not the ideal place for naked flames, especially when sleeping. The Aroma-Care capsule machine is designed to fill your bedroom with sleep-inducing aromas without worrying about setting fire to your bed! Go to Aroma-Care.com to purchase your machine for around $89 with eight capsules that will give you ten uses per capsule. Additional capsules cost around $10 and are available in lavender, peppermint, orange, and many other appealing blends.

3) NuCalm: This clinically developed system will help your mind and body relax in minutes and help you drift off to sleep. There are four different aspects to their technology that can be used separately or together to promote relaxation and ease stress and anxiety.

> **• Stimulation Patches**: These are tiny patches of material that, when placed behind the ear, will begin the relaxation process.

> **• Headphones**: These Bluetooth headphones are programmed with a popular sleep-music app from the same company called ReNu that uses binaural tones and acoustic music to soothe your brain and allow you to enter a more relaxing phase.

> **• The Eye Mask:** These comfortable eye masks are one of the most effective on the market and completely block out all light.

> **• Topical Creams or Pastilles:** These structured dietary aids are packed with ingredients that help the body to calm down and reach a natural state of relaxation.

4) Good Support Pillows: There are multiple options when it comes to pillows, as we discussed earlier, according to different sleeping positions, and they can be as simple as that adjust to your neck and shoulders shape. This type of technological smart pillow is designed by experts like the Medzena Counter-Memory Foam Orthopedic pillow designed after providing treatment to thousands of neck and shoulder pain patients.

5) Whole-Body Magnetic Resonance Wheel: If you have room in your home for a 6ft vertical loop and you are prepared to spend $3000 upward and pay a monthly subscription of $80, then this is the tech for you! The Magnesphere is an impressive piece of kit that is marketed as the ultimate stress reducer. Sitting inside its giant loop and being bombarded with a series of magnets is the perfect way to improve your heart rate variability, which helps you deal with stress, or so the experts tell us. If you are sitting on the fence with this idea, it may help you to know that the New England Patriots have one, and if it's good enough for the Patriots, then who are we to argue?

6) Muse S Headband: From the expensive magnetic loop to one of the cheaper pieces of tech on the market. For just $2, you can try this classy-looking headband that gives you feedback on your brain activity, your heart rate, and other movements that control your feature responses to sleep. It has a comforting audio feature that gives you gentle prompts and suggestions to help you prepare for a good night's rest.

7) Chilling Pad for Your Bed: This type of sleep system is designed to help people who have trouble naturally adjusting their body temperature. We all know how difficult it can be to fall asleep with cold feet or how uncomfortable sweating in bed can be. For around $500, you can purchase a system from chilitechnology.com with a hydro-powered mattress pad filled with water and controlled by remote controls. This means that both sides of the bed can be regulated to suit the individual sleeper's temperature requirement.

8) Embr Wave Bracelet: If you do find temperature regulation a problem, but you don't want to use a pad, this unintrusive piece of tech will help you adjust your body temperature by wearing a simple bracelet. It measures the core temperature and then uses stimulating sensations inside the wrist to warm or cool the body depending on the wearer's requirements.

9) Sound Machines: Not everyone likes earplugs when dealing with sleep in a noisy environment, so these machines give you a more subtle option. It listens to your environment and adjusts the audio volume to mask any sounds that may obstruct your sleep. It has a sleep timer that turns off the volume as you fall asleep.

NATURAL METHODS OF INDUCING SLEEP

Over-the-counter sleep medications may seem like a good idea to help you fall asleep and are often marketed as a natural solution. Some brands may seem helpful, but they are filled with antihistamines and can prevent you from feeling alert and wakeful upon waking, which negatively impacts you the following day.

SUPPLEMENTS

These supplements will help you get your circadian rhythm aligned and increase your natural responses to daytime and nighttime elements.

1) 5-HTP: Your body uses tryptophan to produce 5-HTP, which is then converted into serotonin. It also aids in the manufacturing of melatonin, which is vital for sleep. As the body ages, both serotonin and melatonin levels will lessen, so 5-HTP is one of the most effective supplements available. High doses can be toxic, so it is important to get the right dosage depending on your overall health and age. A dose of 50mg up to three times a day is generally considered safe for most people

2) GABA: Also known as gamma butyric acid, is a natural compound created in the brain to help us calm our nervous system and aid natural feelings of sleepiness. A dose of 100 mg daily will help improve periods of REM sleep and higher energy levels in the morning

3) L-Theanine: This amino acid is found in green tea and helps increase the production of dopamine, serotonin, and GABA while also counteracting the effects of caffeine. L-theanine also mimics the alpha waves that encourage sleep and helps the brain promote sleep and elevate the mood following a great night's rest

4) Vitamin B6: Deficiency in natural levels of this vitamin is linked to insomnia, so you must have healthy levels. B6 converts the tiny level of natural tryptophan into serotonin, so it is a key part of sleep health. Vitamin B6 is also proven to stimulate the brain during REM sleep, leading to more graphic and memorable dreams during these phases. Suggested doses range from 1.3mg to 1.7 mg daily depending on age and gender

5) Melatonin: Supplements are exactly what they are described as. If you have a low level of a natural element, then you need to supplement your levels. Melatonin is an important factor in sleep, so while it is normally prescribed for jet lag, insomniacs can also benefit from taking controlled doses. A daily dose of 0.5mg to 3mg is ideal for promoting nighttime sleepiness, and higher doses will only prolong those feelings during the day.

6) Kava Kava: The South Pacific Islands' indigenous population has been using this root as a substitute for alcohol for generations. It is said to have all the benefits of alcohol without the side effects. Kava bars are springing up across the US, where you can visit and taste the unique flavors of this drink. The benefits of kava kava for sleep are effective as they reduce stress and improve sleep quality. The recommended rate to consume before bedtime is 250mg

7) CBD Oil: Recent attitudes to CBD oil have changed completely in the last few years. This non-psychoactive extract comes from the cannabis plant but is completely safe to use for other health issues as well as lack of sleep. It helps control symptoms of migraines and arthritis while healing brain trauma and reducing anxiety. The only problem with CBD oil as a sleep enhancer is that the large dosage (around 150mg per day) can be expensive

8) Lemon Balm: This health supplement is available in many different forms and helps the body fall asleep by reducing anxiety and calming stress. It contains the ingredient rosmarinic acid that induces a mild sedative effect and helps sleep.

9) Valerian Root: This supplement is mostly used for treating sleep disorders as it promotes a mild sedative effect on the brain. Doses of between 400mg and 900 mg per day can alleviate insomnia symptoms but should not be taken for a period longer than 20 consecutive days

10) Magnesium: This supplementation is responsible for improved hormonal and electrical waves in elder patients and helps strengthen the nervous system. Magnesium deficiency is common in the developed world, and it is essential to restore healthy levels for quality sleep. The recommended dietary allowance is 310 to 420 mg per day, but some of this will come from food. The suggested dose for supplemental magnesium is 240mg per day.

The key to supplements is to understand when they are needed and their effect on your body. Combining supplements can produce even more effective results, and the combination of GABA and 5-HTP can prove to be one of the best ways to improve sleep quality and duration. The amino acids contained in the supplements will help you fall asleep quickly and for prolonged periods.

10 MORNING HABITS TO BOOST PRODUCTIVITY

Do you love mornings? Do you leap out of bed and greet the world with joy and enthusiasm? Most of us dread getting out of bed in the morning and would rather get back under the covers and reset the alarm for later. However, when you look at the morning routines of some of the most successful people in the world, you will find they are generally early risers who make the most of the day ahead.

Different routines work for different people, so it's important to adopt the habits that suit your lifestyle. These ten habits will give you an idea of what will help you face the day and look forward to mornings rather than dread them.

1) Get up earlier than you need to: It will allow you to have more time for your daily tasks. Avoid rushing and allow yourself to appreciate the new day and feel grateful. It may only be 10 minutes to begin with, but you will feel the difference. Always remember not to start your day with stressful thoughts. Do not use social media or open work email straight after you open your eyes. It will help to avoid a stressful start of the day.

2) Drink lemon water: When you go to bed, place a bottle of water with a slice of lemon in it beside your bed. When you wake up, start the day with a healthy drink and rehydrate your body after a long dry night. It will also help your me-

tabolism and fat burning.

3) Make your bed: Imagine how satisfying it feels to be so organized you return home to a pristine bed ready for sleeping. Just tidying your bed will reduce your anxiety levels and improve your mood.

4) Be mindful: Look out of the window and say thank you to yourself that you are still working hard and will achieve your goals soon. This may feel a bit odd but imagine like you are your own boss and you are giving yourself credit. Seriously this can give you a huge boost in the morning and fill you with joy and positive energy.

5) Shower: Feeling clean will give you a tremendous boost, so when you clean your teeth, make sure you jump in the shower too. Try a tingling menthol shower gel for extra freshness and muscles energy boost.

6) Eat a healthy breakfast: Never skip this important meal. Energy from food is essential, and you can increase your focus and concentration by eating proteins, healthy fats, and grains before you face the day. Try a healthy avocado and poached egg on wholemeal toast to boost your energy levels.

7) Move your body: If the thought of conventional exercise leaves you cold, then try more enjoyable movements. Turn the radio on and dance around your living room for 10 minutes. You will feel the difference, music, and movement are the perfect way to start your day. You could also benefit from singing along and giving your lungs a workout.

8) Yoga: The positions in yoga are perfect fatigue fighters, and doing the downward dog could be perfect for your energy levels.

9) Decide that today is going to be a good day: Say it out loud

and with gusto. Mantras and chants can start your day with a positive spin that will help you become more productive and successful.

10) Get your hard work done in the morning: When you have a list of things to do, it can be tempting to leave the harder tasks until later. Get them done early and you will feel energized and filled with optimism.

CONCLUSION

Now you have the knowledge and the tools to make every night a restful and rejuvenating time. Your moods will improve, your overall health will be better, and you will look at life with a more optimistic outlook. Sleep is the key to happiness, and you are now the holder of that key! Stop overthinking, stop thinking of what people will say, only take care of yourself and your loved ones as your health and sleep for good health is very important. You can bring lots of joys to someone's life (like how I tried to share my experiences in this book), so please keep your energy high by sleeping well. Good luck with your new routine, and here's to successful sleep and all that it brings with it!

Are you having trouble falling asleep, or staying asleep? How many times have you found yourself lying awake at night wondering why you can't get to sleep? How many nights have you been unable to sleep, knowing that you have a busy day ahead of you, but your body and mind still fail to respond to your needs.

Do you want insight into why this happens, and how you can get a better night's sleep every single night? Luckily, you have found the right book!

If you believe that sleep is the most important part of your day, then you will appreciate the tips and hints in this book to help you make the most of your rest. Get the sleep you need, and you will wake every morning with a smile on your face, a positive attitude, and a joyful outlook on life. Download this book now and to get some restful sleep tonight!

Author: Abdur Rashid
Msc (Public Health) MCSP
Consultant Neuro-spinal & Musculoskeletal physiotherapist
Abdur is a well-known physiotherapist based in Scotland UK